ATLANTIC FLYWAY

FLYWAY

Cy La Tour

THE
Bird Watcher's
Guide

by HENRY HILL COLLINS, JR.

Illustrated with Photographs

Line Drawings and Cover by RICHARD HARKER

GOLDEN PRESS NEW YORK

TABLE OF CONTENTS

*ART CREDITS: James Gordon Irving, birds on endsheets, pp. 42-43
Arthur Singer, p. 7.*

The quetzal, a now-rare trogon of Central America, was sacred to the Mayan Indians.

BECOMING A BIRD WATCHER

Birds have fascinated mankind since the dawn of history. Their power of flight stirs our imagination and our envy. Their songs and plumage delight us with their beauty. The great sweep and rhythm of their migrations fill us with wonder. We marvel at their courtship, their nest-building, and how they incubate their eggs and raise their young.

Legend has many stories about birds. The ancient Egyptians worshiped a bird-god, Horus, who had the head of a falcon and the body of a man. The quetzal, a beautiful red-and-green bird of Central America, was sacred to the Maya. Tradition tells how the cries of geese once awoke a garrison of early Rome in time to save the city from the Gauls.

The Bible often speaks of birds: "The way of an eagle in the air . . .";

"Are not five sparrows sold for two farthings, and not one of them is forgotten before God?"; "... Foxes have holes, and birds of the air have nests; but the Son of man hath not where to lay his head."

Centuries after Christ, kings and nobles trained hawks to hunt other birds and small animals; and the ancient art of falconry reached its height of popularity.

In the struggles following the Crusades, the Saracens demanded and received Greenland gyrfalcons as ransom for captured Christian nobles.

In 1492, land birds that Columbus saw migrating southwestward over the Atlantic encouraged him to keep on, despite the protests of his crews. Five days later he sighted land, and discovered a new world. History is filled with stories like these about birds.

Our language and culture, too, are full of references to birds. "Black as a crow," "thin as a rail," "Mother Goose," and "dead as a dodo" are common phrases. The bald eagle is our national emblem. The turkey symbolizes our day of Thanksgiving. The Baltimore oriole and cardinal have lent their names to famous baseball teams.

In a magnificent wave of song, the spring chorus of robins can be heard across the country in the early hours of dawn. The evening melody of the hermit thrush haunts us with its beauty.

It is small wonder many of us like to watch and listen to birds, and want

The Bayeux tapestry shows Earl Harold setting out for France with his hawk and hounds.

Bartlett Hendricks—National Audubon Society

Being out at sunrise on a summer morning is just one of the many joys of bird watching.

to learn more about them. Bird watching, indeed, is a hobby enjoyed by young and old, men and women, outdoor-lovers and shut-ins. This book tells how you can become a bird watcher.

You can watch birds all year, without a license and without paying any fees. You can watch them alone, or with others; by day or by night; on land or on sea; for a moment, or an hour, or as long as you wish.

The sport of bird watching has no innings, quarters, or sets. It does not have to be called on account of rain, or cold, or darkness. It is an interest that can last a lifetime, and one that yields pleasure and profit all the while. Few people who have watched a bird once through binoculars will

lay down those binoculars for good.

Bird watching, however, does not necessarily require binoculars or any other special equipment. They help, of course; but much of the pleasure of the hobby comes from using your unaided ear and eye. The mellow notes of the bluebird, the song of a vireo, the sight of wild geese overhead—any of these will bring back to you, throughout your life, memories of melting snowbanks in spring, lazy summer afternoons, or brisk days in the field in fall.

These, then, are some of the joys of bird watching — joys that the breath of time cannot tarnish. These are some of the reasons why people become bird watchers.

You can start the hobby by going

out almost anywhere and looking for birds. Near your own home you will often find the familiar robin, song sparrow, house sparrow, jay, crow, or pigeon. Then you can go to a nearby park, or the country, or the seashore to see other species. As you learn more you may want to go still farther afield. Indeed, an interest in birds has taken some persons to the foothills of the Himalayas and to some of the most remote islands on the globe.

You will be surprised, once you begin to look for birds, at how many you will see. Some you may not recognize. An experienced bird watcher can help you identify these, or you can look them up in a book. Once you begin watching birds, you will have a wonderful hobby that continually lends itself to the enjoyment of your surroundings. The world about you will have a different look; your ears will hear sounds they never heard before.

The new bird watcher has many subjects from which he can choose.

Mary Tremaine

An interest in birds has led many birds watchers to exotic spots on the globe. They hope to see and to identify scores of new species of birds for their life lists.

Commuters in the New York City area can see nesting mute swans from their train windows.

He can study bird identification or bird songs. He can learn how to attract birds to his home or garden. He can go on bird trips and take up some of the sporting aspects of bird watching. He can help with bird censuses, study bird migration and other bird behavior, or work to become an ornithologist. He can photograph or band birds. He can protect them by preserving their habitat and helping in other conservation projects. He can enjoy the society of other bird watchers in a bird club. Bird watching is a pleasant, informal way to meet people of similar interests either at home or when traveling. Members of local bird clubs almost always welcome an out-of-town birder to their meetings and field trips.

Ornithology, or the study of birds, is an important branch of zoology. It is a highly developed biological science. But so vast is the field, and comparatively so little of it is yet known, that the amateur has many opportunities to help add to our knowledge. Amateurs have made excellent and detailed studies of the life histories of common birds. They also work with experts in investigation of certain migration and population problems. In the pages that follow we will point out the various aspects of bird watching, and will show how an amateur can enjoy them either for sport or for science.

Telescopes and binoculars are useful aids to bird watchers.

EQUIPMENT FOR BIRD WATCHING

Binoculars

Binoculars, or "bird glasses," though not absolutely necessary, are a great help in identifying and studying birds.

Since any magnification is better than none, some beginners may use low-powered, non-prismatic opera glasses or field glasses. Such glasses have limited fields of view, and no separate adjustment for the two eyes.

If you decide to get binoculars, you should consider carefully the type you buy. Binoculars differ in various ways, notably in magnification, field, and illumination. Magnification is always the first figure stamped on the cover plate. Thus a 7 x 35 glass magnifies the object seven times. The second figure refers to the diameter of the lens farthest from the eye, or objective lens, measured in millimeters. The larger the figure, the larger is this lens, which determines the amount of light received. Thus a 7 x 50 has a lens 15 mm. wider than a 7 x 35 (but actually admits more than twice the light, because it is the *area* of the lens that counts).

In choosing a glass, bear in mind these factors:

Magnification: The larger the image, the more detail is visible; but also, the greater the magnification, the greater the "wandering" of the object being viewed, because of the motion of the hands holding the glasses. Binoculars with magnification above 8 are difficult for many people to hold steady; they are usually used on a tripod or on some other kind of support.

Field: The larger the field, or area seen through the glasses, the easier it is to locate a moving bird, or find where it landed.

Light transmission: The more light that comes through, the easier it is to see the bird. Binoculars that have most of their glass surfaces coated with magnesium fluoride transmit 50 per cent more light than do uncoated glasses.

Reliability: Many binoculars sold in stores may be out of adjustment because of rough handling during shipment. Buy only from a responsible dealer who will give you a guarantee that the glass is in adjustment and free of defects. Try to find out if repair parts are available. Insist on a trial outdoors.

Binoculars may be the most valuable birding equipment you will use. Get the best you can afford, and treat them carefully.

Binocular lenses magnify the image. The larger the magnification, the more detail is visible.

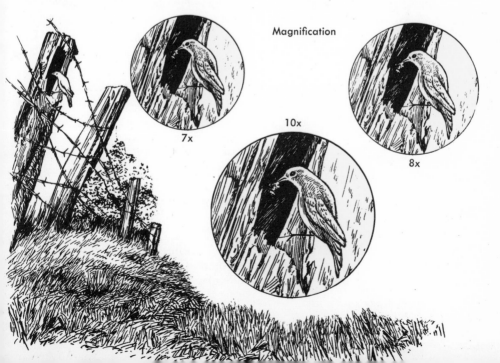

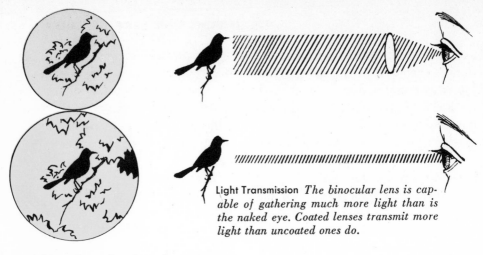

Light Transmission *The binocular lens is capable of gathering much more light than is the naked eye. Coated lenses transmit more light than uncoated ones do.*

Field *These binoculars have the same magnification; the lower glass has a larger field.*

PRINCIPAL TYPES OF BINOCULARS

Beginners:	6 x 30	Best for convenient handling. Has widest field, except for special wide-angle models.
	7 x 35	Best all-around glass.
	8 x 40	Shows more detail than the above; but also more difficult to keep steady, and heavier to hold.
Advanced:	8 x 30	Compact and light in weight, but with low light transmission.
	7 x 50	Maximum light transmission. Twice as large and heavy as the 7 x 35. Best for poor lighting conditions.
	9 x 35	Combines high power with moderate size and satisfactory light transmission. Requires experienced handling.
	10 x 50 and 12 x 50	Satisfactory only for skilled birders. Requires very steady holding. Often used on a tripod or other stand.
Special Purpose:	7 x 35— super-wide field	Shows almost twice the area of standard models. Very heavy. Caution: many poorly constructed models are on the market; badly corrected for optical error.
	6 x 25— pocket-wide field	Good glass for birder who wants glass with him at all times. Other smaller pocket models are usually of poor quality.

Center-focusing Glasses

Center-focus models are preferred for birding, because of the ease and speed with which range can be adjusted. To adjust center-focus binoculars initially, look at the letters on a sign about 300 feet away:

1. First bend the center hinge till you see only a single round picture.

2. Close your right eye, and look through the binoculars with your left eye. Move the center focusing wheel until you can read the letters on the sign clearly.

3. Now close your left eye and look at the sign, through the binoculars, with your right eye. Adjust the right eye focus by turning the moveable eyepiece until the sign is sharp and clear. This one adjustment should make your right eye equal to your left whenever you use the binoculars.

4. Now try with both eyes. If the sign is not quite clear, repeat the whole process, slowly, from the beginning.

Remember: every time you move the center wheel, you are adjusting *both* eyepieces. The right eyepiece should be adjusted separately, and only once. After the right eyepiece has been properly focused, the scale at its base will indicate *your* best setting (the number directly above the fixed white line). Remember this number.

Always use the binoculars with the right eyepiece set at this point. All adjustments for near or distant focus will be made with the center wheel.

The focus is the same for all distances beyond 50 to 80 feet from your eyes and on out as far as you can see. You will make most of your adjustments in order to view birds closer than 50 feet. By screwing the center focus wheel clockwise, as far as possible, you will be able to see through the binoculars at their shortest possible range.

If you have a chance to choose between several binoculars, try to obtain the one through which you can see most clearly at the closest range.

A store specializing in binoculars, with its own repair shop, can make certain binoculars adjust more closely than when they came from the factory. This can be done without dam-

Center-focusing Binoculars

Both eyepieces can be adjusted at one time on these glasses. They are preferred by most bird watchers because of the speed with which they can be adjusted in the field.

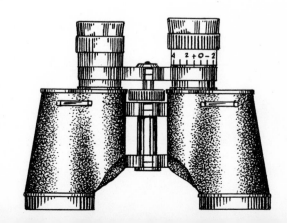

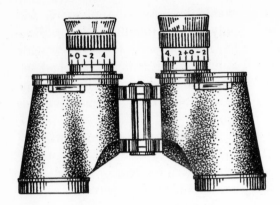

Individual-focusing Binoculars
Each eyepiece on these glasses has to be adjusted separately. Birds often move too fast for the bird watcher to make adjustments for close viewing.

aging the binoculars or affecting the distant focus.

Individual-focusing Binoculars

If you have individual-focus binoculars, just bend the hinge till you see one round picture, as described before.

Have the eyepieces screwed out as far as possible. Screw in one side at a time, to get the clearest focus for each eye on a sign about 300 feet away. Individual-focus binoculars are marked on both eyepieces, so that you can mark or memorize your best settings for distant viewing. To view birds at close range, you will have to screw the eyepieces out again; but the birds often move too fast for this to be practical.

Using Binoculars

Persons who wear eyeglasses regularly should have their binoculars fitted with shallow caps; otherwise the field is considerably reduced.

When birding with binoculars, first find your bird with the naked eye. It is extremely difficult to locate a bird through binoculars alone, except when "sweeping" an open area or a body of water. Having located the bird with your eyes, now look at it through your binoculars. Move the wheel a little to get a sharp focus. Remember: beyond approximately 75 feet the best setting will be the same for all ranges.

Even though a bird can be clearly seen with the naked eye, beginners often have trouble locating it in the binoculars. It may help to pick out some feature of the landscape near the bird, such as a dead branch or telephone wire. Look through the binoculars till you find this feature; then find the bird.

On a body of water, a quick glance with the naked eye will locate the more obvious birds. Now take your binoculars and slowly "sweep" the surface of the water and shoreline from left to right. You will probably find many more birds.

Birds move so fast that most birders, as long as they are actively birding, keep their glasses out of their leather cases. However, a sound precautionary measure is always to keep the binoculars on the strap around your neck, to avoid dropping them. When walking or climbing slip the strap under one arm.

In warm weather, when most persons are coatless, the leather case can be used to carry a field guide, notebook, and field card.

Binoculars are valuable precision instruments and deserve to be treated with care. Don't drop, scratch, or bump them. Keep them out of sand and mud. If the lenses seem cloudy, first blow off loose dust, then wipe them very gently with a clean surface of cleansing tissue. You may moisten the tissue with water, but never put water on the lens itself!

In case of rain, a leather rain guard for the eyepieces is a useful accessory. It can be fitted to slide loosely on the neck strap.

A good birder remembers where he puts his binoculars. Never set them on the hood, top, or trunk of a car. Many a birder has lost his glasses when the car drove away!

Do not leave binoculars in a very warm place, such as in the sun or on a radiator. The heat may cause separation of the achromatic lenses—which will make shiny spots or "snowflakes" appear. Should this happen, or if your glasses are otherwise out of adjustment so that they cause eyestrain, or are dirty inside, or fail to function in any manner, do not try to take them apart or repair them yourself. Take them to a qualified repair shop which has a precision collimator.

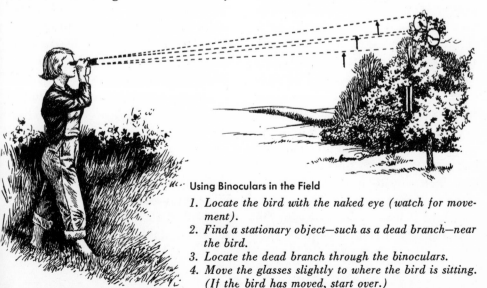

Using Binoculars in the Field

1. *Locate the bird with the naked eye (watch for movement).*
2. *Find a stationary object—such as a dead branch—near the bird.*
3. *Locate the dead branch through the binoculars.*
4. *Move the glasses slightly to where the bird is sitting. (If the bird has moved, start over.)*

Cy La Tour

A car window mount for a telescope is useful for winter birding at the shore.

Telescopes

A spotting telescope is essential for birding at long range—over broad bodies of water, impassable swamps, and sometimes on private property.

A 20x telescope with an objective lens of 40 mm. or more is best. The finer telescopes have internal prismatic adjustments, and interchangeable eyepieces. Some can be equipped with turrets to hold a choice of eyepieces. A selection of eyepieces from 15x up to 40x are suitable for birding. With higher powers the field becomes too small, the light inadequate, and any vibrations due to wind or distortion due to heat shimmer become too great.

A bird is usually located with the lowest power of the three-piece tur-

ret, and then brought closer with the highest power.

To handle a telescope properly, you must have a steady tripod. Be sure to avoid the temptation of buying one that is too light. In any kind of wind, a sturdy tripod is essential. One with an adjustable head is preferable; and an elevator attachment is also excellent, to move the telescope up and down. Car window mounts are desirable, too, especially for winter birding by the sea.

Unless the telescope has a "boss" to attach it directly to the tripod, you will need a special adapter.

Wherever you buy your telescope, be sure to get full instructions with it, and insist on the privilege of a trial period.

Your Field Guide

Several good field guides are listed on page 118. Such books have colored pictures of the birds and text that tells of their habits, habitat, and voice, and their "field marks," or special points that distinguish one species from another in the field. Any birder must have a good field guide.

A Field Check List

A pocket "field card" lists all the birds that occur annually in a certain area. Many state and local bird clubs prepare their own cards or know where a suitable card for the area can be obtained. In quantities of 25 or more they usually cost only a few cents apiece.

A field check list is a convenient way of keeping a record of the species seen or heard on a bird trip. In tallying up at the end of the trip, note total numbers (or estimates) of individuals, as well as the various species, seen or heard. This will give some idea of the relative abundance of the different species.

The Field Notebook

Carry a field notebook to write down your observations. If the book is looseleaf and one page is used for each species, these pages can be torn out after the trip and filed by species or groups in your permanent filing system. If you see a bird you cannot identify, write down all the data you can concerning it at the time. Memory of such details fades fast.

A Home Library

After you have a good field guide, next get a book on life histories of birds, and then one on the birds of your own state. Most states now have a state bird book. Later, add a book on bird songs, another on migration, and a basic textbook on ornithology. There are hundreds of bird books. Plan to build a well-rounded bird watcher's library. A few basic volumes are listed on pp. 118-122.

Bird Records

A good way to learn bird songs, apart from hearing them in the field, is by listening to bird records. Several long-playing releases are now available. They will permit you to hear over and over again phrases that are difficult to remember, as well as those distinctive and joyous songs you may hope you will never forget.

Telescopes are helpful for seeing shore birds, such as black skimmers, across a bay.

Helen Cruickshank—National Audubon Society

FIRST STEPS IN BIRD WATCHING

You can start bird watching as soon as you go outside, or simply by re-examining the world from your window. Look around at trees and shrubs, telephone wires and TV antennas; sweep the ground and sky with your gaze. Listen as you look. You may see or hear a bird almost instantly.

When you do, if you are outside, approach the bird slowly, noiselessly, and *straight ahead*. Birds are easily frightened by sideways move-

ments, but often seem to be poor judges of distance.

After a few steps, stop and study the bird. If you have binoculars, look at it through them. Notice its *habitat*. Is the bird on the ground, on the water, in a shrub, or on a tree? If it is in a tree, how high up is it?

What are the bird's *habits*? Is it walking, hopping, climbing a tree? Is it singing or calling? What does its *voice* sound like? When you have

20

Mary Tremaine

Birding is a sport you can enjoy alone or with friends. Working out your own identifications of the birds you see will give you a great sense of accomplishment.

You can watch birds for just a few minutes at a time, if you wish. You can take a short stroll and watch birds before breakfast, at noon, or after work. Or you can study the birds seen from your window. On weekends or free days you can go on longer bird trips.

You will soon become more aware of birds. Going to work, you will notice crows along the parkway, ducks from the train window, pigeons or gulls flying over the city. Whatever you are doing, you will tend to be on the lookout for birds.

Finding a Field Companion

It will be helpful for you, as a beginner, to go out when you can with a veteran bird watcher. He can show you how to find birds, what to look for in them, and how to tell one species from another.

Your local Audubon Society or bird club has many veteran birders as members. Ask one of them to take you on a bird walk. The club probably also has regular field trips, on which newcomers are welcome. Ask to go on one. Get all the help you can from old-timers.

On the other hand you can go out

seen all you can at that distance, walk up closer and study it again.

When you get too near, the bird will fly off. As it does, notice its silhouette and manner of flight.

If you have a field guide with you, look up the bird right away. But make sure that the bird you think you have identified occurs in your part of the country, and at that season. When you have decided on the species, write down the date and place you saw it. This is how you start your "life list" (see p. 59).

by yourself equally well. You can do this any time, anywhere. You don't have to wait for holidays, weekends, or a scheduled field trip. And it is the best way to learn about birds, and to consolidate what a veteran bird watcher may have told you.

There is a great sense of accomplishment, too, in making your own identifications, in deciding for yourself whether you have really seen that particular species of sparrow, warbler, or hawk. But be cautious. Don't put down a bird on your list until you are sure you are right. You can ruin your reputation as a bird watcher by careless or inaccurate identifications.

Go out in the field all you can—with others or alone. It is fun to get out, and it is the best way to become a good bird watcher.

What to Wear

When watching birds about your own home or in a local park, you can wear ordinary city clothes. On a regular bird trip, however, wear sturdy old clothes, light in summer, warm in winter; and comfortable shoes that you won't mind getting wet.

Bird watchers are a motley crew. Each has his own theory as to the best headgear, underwear, and footwear. You will probably develop your own theories, too. Extra equipment in summer might include a cap and dark glasses. In cold weather, a scarf,

long underwear, ear muffs, extra socks, and galoshes may also be desirable. Some of the new quilted clothing developed for the Army and currently used by skiers is very warm and very light in weight. Birding involves a lot of standing around to watch, and you can't always get out of the wind. So, dress warmly.

Some bird watchers carry folded plastic raincoats on all-day trips. These may also be used for protection against cool winds.

Studying Birds from Books

It is well, early in the game, to learn the names of the kinds of birds you can expect to see in your locality at a given time of year. Your bird club may have issued a local list showing the seasonal occurrence and relative abundance of birds in your area, or there may be a state or regional list available.

Look up the birds on this list in your field guide (see p. 118). Learn how to identify them. Study them also in other books that deal with life histories and habits. The more knowledge you can bring with you to the field, the easier it will be to identify the birds you see, and the more fun it will be to watch them.

On your return from a bird trip, look up the birds you have seen, and read all you can about them. The armchair bird watcher gets his quota of enjoyment, too.

Pattern: wing bars?
special color patch on head and neck?

Color: principal color?
breast? wings? tail?

Size: crow? sparrow?

Silhouette: body long? crest?
bill thick? tail rounded?

These are some of the identification marks to look for when you see a bird. This is a blue jay.

HOW TO IDENTIFY BIRDS

In bird watching, the first task is to identify the bird. The sooner you learn identification marks, the sooner you can start making observations about birds.

What to Look For

Here are some of the things to look for when trying to identify a bird:

Size: Is the bird the size of a spar-row, a robin, a pigeon, or a crow? Or is it larger? Or is it somewhere between the sizes of two of these?

Silhouette: What shape is the bird? Is its body long and narrow, or short and plump? Does it have a crest? Is its bill thin or thick? Does it have long legs, a long neck, long bill, or long tail? Is its tail squared, rounded, or pointed?

Does it have a "hunched-up" appearance when perched? Are its wings broad or narrow in flight?

Color: What is the *principal* color of the bird? What color is its cap, head, throat, breast, belly, back, wings, tail? Or its eye, bill, legs, feet? You would be unusually lucky to see all these details, but try to get the color of at least two or three parts of its body.

Pattern: Does the bird have a white wing patch or wing bars? Does it have white outer tail feathers? Or are only the outer corners of the tail white or yellow? Is the under part of its tail white, yellow, or chestnut? Does the bird have a white or yellow rump?

Are there stripes on the bird's crown, bars on its back, streaks or spots on its breast? Does it have a special color patch on its cheek, ear, or neck? Usually you won't get a chance to note the bird's complete color pattern, but try to get as many details as you can. The more you

remember or write down, the easier it will be for you to identify the bird.

Flight: Is the bird's flight level? Or does it undulate gently; or go up and down in steep, roller-coaster curves? Does the bird zigzag; fly in broad sweeps; or wheel and turn high in the air?

Does the bird fly out from a perch after insects and then fly back again? Does it flutter a lot; fly low over the water; have fast or slow wing beats; spiral upward to a great height on currents of warm air? These flight patterns help in identification. In addition, one of the joys of bird watching is the aesthetic pleasure in watching bird flight.

Conspicuous marks in flight: Many birds show what we call "flight marks"—marks that are seen only in flight. Examples are a white rump, wing stripe, wing patch, or outer tail feathers. Look for special flight marks in any bird you see.

Silhouette in flight: Most species

Individual flight patterns: (l. to r.) flicker, undulating flight; goldfinch, roller-coaster flight; kingbird, flies out from perch after insects, then back to perch.

Learn birds' ranges. You would not expect to see a white ibis except in the South.

of birds have a distinctive silhouette in flight: a "keeled," boat-shaped tail; "fingered" flight feathers; neck stretched out or drawn in. Sometimes the differences in silhouette between species are rather subtle. But by observing the combination of flight pattern, silhouette, and flight marks, most large birds can be identified on the wing, often at the limit of visibility.

Flocks: Some birds fly singly or in pairs; others, in small groups; still others, in flocks. You can often identify the latter by their collective appearance. Does the flock fly in a wedge behind a leader; in long lines low over the ocean; in large irregular bunches? Or is it so tightly organized that it turns and wheels in unison, seemingly without a leader?

Field marks: Each species of bird has its own "field marks," by which it can be differentiated in the field from all other species. Often one mark is sufficient for positive identification. Does the bird, for example, have light legs or dark; black or gray underwings? Is its lower bill yellow or black? Does it have a thick conical bill or a thin sharp bill; a buffy wash on its breast; streaks on its back?

Sometimes two marks are necessary to clinch the identification. Does the bird have a yellow rump *and* a thin bill; are its legs and bill *both* yellow; does it have a reddish cap *and* a white line over the eye?

Learn and look for the field marks.

Characteristic habits: On alighting, does the bird pump its tail? Does it "freeze" motionless in the marsh with its bill pointed skyward? Does it jump up straight from the water into flight, or does it patter along the surface before taking off?

Range, Season, and Habitat

The inexperienced birder, when he sees a bird he cannot immediately identify, in most instances should automatically exclude from consideration those species that would be out of their range, season, or habitat, at that time or place. He thus narrows down the possibilities by eliminating impossible or highly improbable species.

He should study the distribution of birds, the seasonal occurrence of birds, and birds' preferred habitats. He should consider only the species that might normally be found in that range and habitat at that time.

Rarities, of course, may turn up anywhere at any time. They may be blown off course or away from home by hurricanes, strong on-shore or off-shore winds. Or they may be induced to wander by hunger or disease. Finding rarities is one of the exciting things about birding. But the beginner should not take the responsibility of identifying and reporting unusual species unaided.

Identification by Voice

Just as we recognize different people by their voices, so we can recognize different kinds of birds by their voices. Each species has its characteristic song, call, cry, and alarm note. Most of these sounds are quite distinctive.

A beginner with a good ear can learn many bird notes with little effort. He can learn to identify a song by tracing the sound until he sees the bird that is making it. Or he can ask a veteran birder to teach him to iden-

Group flight patterns: (l. to r.) ducks in long lines; Canada geese in V-shaped migration flight; "explosion" from the ground of bobwhites.

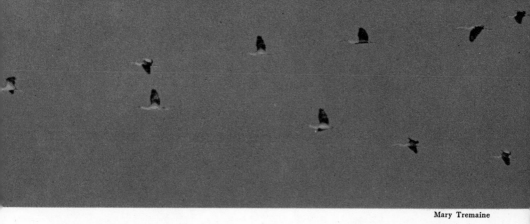

Scarlet ibis of northern South America fly in a perfect V-shaped flight pattern.

tify bird calls in the field. Or he can study bird songs at home from records.

A trained observer can identify most birds as accurately by sound as by sight. Indeed, sometimes he *must* hear a bird to identify it. Certain crows, meadowlarks, and flycatchers can be safely named *only* if heard. The different species of these look too much alike to be identified solely by appearance.

In fact, the skilled birdman frequently identifies birds more quickly by sound than by sight. A bird can be hidden in the leaves or in the reeds of a marsh; but if it gives voice, the trained birder can tell what kind it is. The dim light of dawn or dusk is no barrier to such an identification, nor is the blackness of midnight.

In a spring dawn the old hand can step outside his house in the suburbs, or listen by his open window, and identify a dozen birds in two minutes. Without craning his neck to see treetop warblers, he can note their presence by their songs as he strolls along a woodland path. The good bird watcher is also a bird listener.

Identification Problems

Often when you see a bird, it is too far away, the light is too dim, or your glance is too brief to permit you to tell what species it is. Sometimes all you can put down on your list is "scaup," "hawk," "small flycatcher," "(sp.?)"—meaning "species uncertain." Sometimes you can't put down anything at all.

With practice you will be able to distinguish birds you would have thought it impossible to tell apart a few weeks before. The more species you identify, the easier bird recognition becomes. Soon you will no longer be astonished when an old-timer names, by the angle of its wings, a bird flying low over the distant horizon. In time you may be making the same identification yourself.

HOW TO FIND BIRDS

Some people say they never see any birds. But when a veteran bird watcher takes such a person out and asks him to point out some birds, he usually can find a good number. So if you, as a beginner, *try* to locate birds, you too may be surprised at how many you will find.

Where to Look

The veteran, of course, has learned certain tricks. He slowly scans the landscape looking for the most conspicuous birds—those in flight. Then he looks at all trees and bushes to see if he can catch a glimpse of any movement or if any patch of twigs is stirring. If so, it may be astir with a bird.

He examines the tops of trees, buildings, and cliffs to see if any birds are silhouetted against the sky. If a marsh lies in front of him, he scans it carefully for herons or egrets. When these birds stand upright, they look like sticks when seen from a distance. Or he looks for a patch of white that may betray the presence of an egret or a gull.

The veteran does the same if there is a lawn before him, or a meadow, a field, a fairway, or a runway. Careful study of an area will often reveal one or more birds running over the ground, or perhaps standing motionless doing their own surveying.

As you keep on watching birds, you will pick up these and other tricks. Look around all the time. Birds move fast; every minute, indeed, every few seconds, the birds in the space about you have moved and the bird life presents a different picture. With every step you enter a slightly different environment and new birds will come into view.

All this may sound pretty obvious, but some people, even on a bird walk, tend to stare at their feet, or at the path ahead. If you want to see birds, look at the world about you; let your feet take care of themselves.

Don't forget also to keep sweeping the sky, and from time to time look behind you. Keen eyes can spot wedges of flying geese at a great distance. Birds fly so fast that, if you don't keep looking back at intervals, they will be in the sky above you and gone before you can get your glasses on them.

Once you have located a bird, find it in your binoculars and try to identify it. Observe it as long as you can, and pay particular attention to its habits. These not only help in identification but are of interest in the study of behavior.

The Audubon Society's Theodore Roosevelt Memorial Sanctuary in Long Island, New York, is a fine place to watch bird behavior.

Sweeping Open Areas with Binoculars

Sweeping open areas slowly with your glasses will often yield surprising results. Such spaces may include bodies of water, rivers, plains, deserts, tundra, golf courses, beaches, and mud flats.

Start at one side of the horizon and work your way slowly across the field of vision to the other. If the area is, like the ocean, very large, you may want to try it with several depths of focus. Stop and study carefully any strange-looking objects. You will often find birds that you cannot see with the naked eye.

Most bird watchers have found this technique to be so effective in locating birds that they automatically sweep every open area, whether it be water or land.

When a group is birding by car, the driver often stops momentarily by an open place to give each occupant a chance to roll down his window and sweep his sector of the horizon.

"Squeaking" and Mimicking

While sweeping permits you to study birds at a distance, "squeaking" sometimes brings the birds to you. In order to squeak, simply stay still and kiss the back of your hand or fingers. Sometimes you can actually get a dozen or more birds to come toward you to investigate this noise. Don't move. Vary the squeaking sounds. The birds will continue to come and inspect you for quite some time.

One theory about this noise is that the squeaking sounds like young birds and hence attracts the adults.

You may spot a motionless egret by "sweeping" a marsh area with your binoculars.

Mary Tremaine

Helen Cruickshank—National Audubon Society

A sudden loud noise made by banging a pan or throwing a rock will sometimes bring out gallinules and other secretive marsh birds. This is a purple gallinule.

The method does seem to work best in or near the breeding season.

Artificial bird calls, on sale at many places where bird houses, seed, etc. are sold, as well as in bookstores and elsewhere, make a variety of sounds. They also are good for squeaking up birds. After long use, some have to be rejuvenated by inserting a little rosin in the squeaking cavity.

In addition to squeaking, many bird watchers try to imitate the notes of various birds in order to attract them. Chickadees, goatsuckers, bobwhites, owls, and other species often respond to human imitations.

"Owlers," bird watchers who specialize in the study or calling of owls, sometimes develop great skill as mimics. Some owls, answering an imitation of their notes, will actually swoop down and graze the head of the "owler." Others in the woods will keep up an exchange of hoots with a good owl-caller for a long time.

Some persons learn to mimic dozens of different species with exceptional skill, and, when hidden by bushes, frequently deceive fellow bird watchers.

"Raising" Birds

A "whooshing" noise with the mouth, made by exhaling rhythmically with the upper lip overhanging the lower, will often bring several

A good place to see migrating warblers without getting a "warbler neck" is a spot on a hill-side where you can be on a level with the tops of trees. But some species, such as this yellow warbler, may feed and nest in low shrubs.

hidden land birds out into the open.

A pre-dawn bird watcher usually carries a powerful flashlight. This is useful for locating a breeding bird on a known nest. If the nest is high, you can sometimes just see the bird's tail sticking out over the edge. A flashlight is also useful for spotting a screech owl at its entrance hole in a tree trunk, or for startling a barn owl from its roost in an old tower.

A sudden loud noise in a fresh-water marsh will often set previously silent rails and gallinules to jabbering. Hand clapping, throwing pebbles, and banging on a tin dish are favorite ways to "wake up the marsh."

Good Seeing Locations

Keep the sun at your back for the best view of birds. Try to arrange the course of your bird trips so that, if you are traveling east and west, you will go west in the morning, east in the afternoon.

In looking for warblers and other species that are most often seen in the tops of trees, try to find a hillside path, raised causeway, viaduct or aqueduct, bridge, hilltop, building, or fire-tower where you can be on a level with the treetops. It is easier to identify treetop species when you can get close enough to see them readily.

Listening for Birds

As a bird watcher you will also soon become a bird listener. You will be able to locate and to identify birds by their voices.

To find birds by their voices, stay still and listen. You will often hear birds before you see them, or even when you can't see them at all. If you want to look at a bird that you hear, follow its voice. Soon you ought to be able to locate it.

This is not always easy. Some birds are ventriloquial—they throw their voices. Others such as vireos, which sing on their nests, remain so still and so well hidden amid the foliage that it takes quite a long time to find them.

After you have learned bird songs, you can identify birds by song, and enjoy listening to them, even when you are not in a position to spend any time looking for them. This may be the case when you are on a hike with persons who are not interested in birds, when you are driving through the country, or when you are sitting by an open window.

The "Seat Pleasant"

As you become skilled in bird listening, one of your special pleasures may be to find a "seat pleasant," a favorite rock or log seat where you can listen to birds. Choose a comfortable location near several different habitats. Get there before dawn on a spring morning. See how many different species you can identify by song from that one spot in half an hour or in an hour.

Just listen, listen, listen, and try to identify every song as it comes to you through the morning calm.

A great horned owl "spotted" by a bird watcher's flashlight.

G. Ronald Austing—National Audubon Society

WHERE TO SEE BIRDS

Each bird has its favorite home, or habitat, as the scientist calls it. Where two or more habitats meet, you will find more kinds of birds than in any one habitat alone. Such meeting places are the *edges* of woods, fields, and lawns; roadsides and unkempt property; gardens and orchards.

Other good places to see birds are clearings in woods, areas around deserted buildings in the country, and abandoned fields and pastures. Indeed, in any spot around farms and houses in the suburbs, wherever there is a variety of planting or a varied terrain, you are likely to find birds.

Many species stay near or on water. It will pay, therefore, to visit ponds, pools, lakes, and reservoirs; streams and rivers; fresh-water marshes and swamps; all kinds of beaches, mud flats, and salt marshes;

A variety of terrain and unkempt property provide good birding areas. Look for them near your home.

(their tow paths are exceptionally good places to see birds), and for watercourses that may have paths alongside. The more varied the countryside and the more "edge," the more kinds of birds you will see.

In season, wildlife refuges are excellent areas for birds. Find out the names of the public or private sanctuaries in your region from your local bird club. If you go to such a refuge at the right time of year, you may see more interesting birds at one time and place than you ever thought possible. At a waterfowl refuge, for example, you may see squadron after squadron of ducks or geese dropping from the sky down to the marsh. They make a magnificent sight, and one which you will long remember.

Each habitat has its own quota of bird species. But deep woods, virgin forests, high mountains, and sandy or rocky deserts have relatively few varieties, though these are often of unusual interest.

The bird population of each type of countryside (terrain) varies with the season, with altitude and latitude, and with the climate (moist, semi-arid, or arid). Some terrains have many more species than others. One

bays, harbors, inlets, and the ocean.

In or near cities look for birds in parks, on river banks, in cemeteries, on golf courses, aqueducts, along power line rights-of-way, on dumps, or public land.

Away from Home

If you want to go farther from home, consult a road map. Look for parks or recreational areas, or for bodies of water. Look for canals of the joys of bird watching is know-ing what birds are to be found where, and when; and then going out and finding them.

Planning a Route

The bird watcher should learn the best places for birds in his area. He can then plot routes that will take him to a number of different habitats.

A typical route in moist country might include a fresh-water swamp and stream, low bottomlands, farm-ing country, a dry upland ridge, a reservoir and a fresh-water pond, suburban woods and gardens, and open fields. A typical salt-water route might include a bay, beach, inlet, bayside sand and mud flats, salt marshes, cliffs, pine barrens, and finally, perhaps, artificial impound-ments on a wildlife refuge.

A typical route in arid mountain-ous country might include lowlands along a river, a tributary stream, dry

Roseate spoonbills are found in areas along the Gulf Coast.

Helen Cruickshank—National Audubon Society

Zoos are excellent places to see birds, especially those birds not native to your own country. In some zoos, certain species of birds from the same geographical region, such as a tropical rain forest or a desert, may be displayed together in one large cage.

canyons, sagebrush slopes, pinyon-covered hillsides, a pine forest, burned-over mountainsides, second growth, high-altitude meadows and pastures, evergreens near timberline, and bare mountaintops.

A typical route in wet country in the southern United States might cover low plains, bayous, levees, oxbows; and, near salt water, beaches, bays, and mangrove islands. Other routes can be worked out in other kinds of country anywhere in the world in the same way.

If you have only a short time in an area completely new to you, get advice from a local bird club.

Zoo Populations

Birds can be seen and studied anywhere, any time. To see some of the most interesting living birds, visit the nearest large zoo. Modern zoos try to provide spacious and natural surroundings.

The zoo may have species from all over the world: hawks, vultures, waders, shorebirds, ducks, parrots. It may have rare and unusual birds, and species from remote lands and islands. Perhaps it will have a room of tropical hummingbirds, exquisite gems that are almost unbelievably beautiful.

Museum Specimens

Also visit the natural history museum nearest you. Study its habitat groups, its bird exhibits, and its other mounted specimens. You can learn much about plumages from birds that always stand still, even though they are lifeless and lack the movement and brilliance of living individuals.

If you are puzzled by some bird you saw in the field and could not identify, ask the curator if you may look at some study skins in trays. This is one of the best ways to learn about birds' feather colors. You may often be surprised at the variations in plumage in one species due to differences in age, molt, sex, and season. Bird books cannot possibly illustrate all these variations.

Become a well-rounded bird watcher. When you travel, visit the best places to see birds in the wild, but also visit zoos and museums.

This is especially true when you visit foreign countries. For instance, in Stockholm at a park called the Skansen, you will find a small zoo in which are displayed many of the animals and birds native to Sweden. Take along a European bird guide in English, however. All the labels on the cages are in Swedish!

Many natural history museums have bird exhibits in which you can study specimens at your leisure. Here you can see the variations in plumage within a single species.

Cy La Tour

The violet-green swallow of the western United States, like other swallows, is often seen on sunny days catching insects on the wing.

WHEN
TO SEE
BIRDS

Helen Cruickshank—National Audubon Society

The best time of the day to see or to hear birds is when they are most active. The time varies with different species of birds.

The early morning—dawn and just after—is best for seeing most kinds. On waking, birds start moving about looking for food. They are then easier to see. That is why bird watchers often go out so early.

Birds also sing most vigorously in the early morning. In the middle of the day, when they have stopped singing and are less active, they are harder to find. In the late afternoon, however, they start moving about again, feeding and singing before they go to rest for the night. But they

are seldom as active or as vocal as they were just after dawn.

Fresh-water marsh birds, usually identified by voice, are noisiest at dawn. They are heard less often during the rest of the day, unless it is unusually cool and cloudy.

Warblers and other small insect-eating land birds are best seen in the hours after dawn. They must wait for insects to wake up and move about before they can commence feeding. The sunlight starts both insects and these birds in motion.

Vultures collect in roosts at night in living or dead trees. In the morning they have to wait for the sun to warm the air sufficiently so that it begins rising in big updrafts, or thermals. On these updrafts the birds soar into the sky. They can be seen easily then from afar. Hawks that use thermals must also wait for the air to warm.

Gulls are most conspicuous when they are feeding. Watch them collect when the cook on a ship throws over the scraps from the galley, or when a garbage scow at sea or a garbage truck on land dumps its load. Look for them at any time behind ferryboats or coastwise ships, or around sewer outlets.

Terns are best seen from the shore when there is a school of bait fish in the vicinity, particularly if the school is being attacked by larger fish. The terns feed on the bait fish driven toward the surface. Fishermen often locate schools of fish by watching the terns hovering over the water.

Shorebirds, such as the sandpipers,

sleep at high tide, huddled in compact groups, on shore or on islands. They scatter to feed over mud and sand flats when the water is low. You can observe them most easily when the tide is about half in. They will be moving about then and coming in toward you ahead of the tide.

Goatsuckers and owls are most often seen or heard at night, when they are seeking their prey or calling. Ducks and other waterfowl may be in evidence at any time during the day, but they are apt to be more on the move in early morning and late afternoon.

Hurricanes and bad storms often carry birds hundreds of miles away from their homes or off their usual migration courses. If you want to see rarities, hurry out to beaches and bodies of water after a storm. Also, don't forget to check "land bird traps," as birdmen call patches of trees and vegetation near the ocean.

Great black-backed gulls are a familiar sight in summer along the Maine coast.
Helen Cruickshank—National Audubon Society

Many male birds establish definite territories at the beginning of the nesting season. They sing to warn other males of the same species to keep away, and also to attract mates.

THE VOICES OF BIRDS

Birds make many sounds. These include songs, calls, and alarm notes. Each species has its own sounds, which are different from those of any other species. Bird watchers can learn to distinguish almost every species by its voice.

Many bird songs are so beautiful that hearing them adds much to the joy of bird watching. The male bird is usually the songster, but sometimes the female sings also, as does the female cardinal. Often the female's song is softer than the male's.

Why Birds Sing

The male sings to attract a female. He also sings to proclaim his rights to a certain nesting territory. He sings this "territorial song" from perches that mark the corners of his "property," moving from one perch to another. Such singing serves to warn other males to keep away. Some birds also apparently sing just for the pleasure of singing.

As incubation proceeds, and after the young hatch, the male sings less and less. Later in the season he is heard only at dawn, and then only for short periods. By the time the young leave the nest and the adults are molting, song has almost stopped. In the autumn, some birds sing again. But songs then often seem weaker than the fully developed songs of spring.

Song Differences

Birds frequently have more than one song. Sometimes one is heard at dawn, another later in the day. One song may be short, another longer and more complicated. A bird's song may

SONG SPARROW
Pres, Pres, Pres, Presbyterian

RUFOUS-SIDED TOWHEE
drink your tea—e-e-e-e

also differ slightly in different parts of its range. Some species, like the larks, also have "flight songs."

Each individual bird also has its own voice, just as we do. This voice differs slightly from all others, but the difference is usually too slight for our ears to detect. Occasionally, however, one particular bird may have an outstanding peculiarity in its song, such as a robin with a "cracked voice."

Experts in bird song find that there is much more variation in song within one species than we normally suspect. Aretas A. Saunders of Fairfield, Connecticut, who has spent a lifetime studying bird voices, has recorded 884 variations in the song of the song sparrow.

Other Bird Sounds

In addition to song, birds make a variety of other sounds. They have call notes, alarm notes, notes of protest, notes of warning. Wild turkeys gobble, rails whinny, owls hoot, crows caw, prairie chickens boom.

Some species, thrushes for instance, have flight notes that keep individuals together in night migration. Some birds, such as the black-necked stilt and yellowlegs, act as sentinels. With their loud cries they warn all animals of approaching danger. Many species—the flicker is one—use special notes in courtship.

Learning to recognize birds by voice increases our enjoyment of the outdoors. It permits us to compre-

BLACK-CAPPED CHICKADEE
chicka-dee-dee-dee; FEE-bee

TUFTED TITMOUSE   *peter-peter-peter*

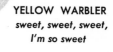

YELLOW WARBLER
sweet, sweet, sweet,
I'm so sweet

CARDINAL
what cheer, what cheer, what cheer

Some birds have songs that can be translated
into English phrases. This makes the songs
easier to remember for many people.

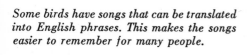

WHITE-THROATED SPARROW
Old Sam PEAbody,
PEAbody, PEAbody

The song of the white-throated sparrow.

hend partially the news broadcasts and weather reports of the wild.

We recognize the mother robin's alarm note that says something is threatening her nest. We understand that all is well when we hear the warbling vireo singing while sitting on its nest. The creaking song of the grackle in the dooryard spruce tells us that snows will soon be gone. The twitter of the chimney swift overhead assures us that warm weather has finally come.

How to Learn Bird Voices

Learning bird voices is helpful in recognizing different species. It is often quicker and easier to identify a bird by sound than by sight.

One way to learn bird voices is to go out on field trips several times with someone who knows them. Another way is to listen over and over again to records of bird songs. The best way, and the way that will implant them in your memory, is to go out and try to figure them out for yourself.

Some people find that they can re-member a bird's song if they learn the English phrases that suggest it. *"Which IS it? Which IS it? Which IS it?"* sings the yellowthroat. *"Pleased, pleased, pleased to MEETcha,"* sings the chestnut-sided warbler. Modern bird guides include as many of these memory-aid phrases as possible.

Bird songs can be written down by using a special system of diagrams which indicate time, pitch, loudness, quality, and phonetics. Such a system is set forth by Mr. A. A. Saunders in his book (p. 119). This method helps the student understand the phrasing and structure of the song and thus makes it easier for him to remember it. Some songs can also be put down in regular musical notation. But this is useful only for a limited number of species.

The fascinating hobby of recording bird voices is open to the advanced bird watcher. Records of the songs of North American birds are far from complete, although the Laboratory of Ornithology at Cornell University, Ithaca, New York, has done much work in this field. Almost nothing has yet been done on recording the bird voices of the tropics, South America, or certain parts of the Old World.

You do not, however, have to be an ornithologist in order to recognize the songs of your local birds. Anyone with good hearing can learn to do so. And when you learn them, a whole new world of enjoyment will open up to you.

A trip to the Hawk Mountain Sanctuary in eastern Pennsylvania during the migration of hawks in the autumn is a special occasion for any bird watcher.

BIRD TRIPS

One of the special joys of bird watching is going on a bird trip. Such a trip may be as short as a half day, or it may be for a week-end, or for an entire vacation.

Likely Localities

Since every locality has its own resident species, the bird watcher can find a good reason for taking a trip almost anywhere. Resorts at the seashore, parks, and mountains are good places to see birds. Trips to these places often are most productive for bird watching in the "off-season" of spring or fall. Rates are lower, crowds are absent, and the weather may be glorious.

The bird watcher also goes to other places especially good for birds. To find them he makes a close inspection of the countryside. He drives along byways and shunpikes; goes out on dead ends to marshes or river banks; finds dirt roads to obscure beaches, mud flats, hidden ponds, and wildlife sanctuaries.

He becomes a specialist in the whereabouts of garbage dumps, sewer outlets, fishing docks, boatyards, power lines, abandoned roads, and old railroads. He takes catwalks through marshes, patrols levees along rivers, and crosses rickety bridges. He follows paths to unimproved corners in cities and suburbs where the

The Wilson's phalarope nests in the prairie regions of North America. The male phalaropes incubate the eggs and take care of the young, reversing the usual order in the bird world. During the breeding season, the females' plumage is more brightly colored than the males'.

wise care, or common negligence, of man has still left a home for birds.

When and Where to Go

Many bird watchers like to make an early start so they can reach their favorite land spots by dawn. This also permits them to go farther afield and avoid heavy traffic. But along the seashore, where tide is more important than time of day, an early start makes less difference.

If you have time for only a half day's trip, the morning is best. On a return trip in midday you will usually miss most heavy traffic. Weekend bird watchers often like to leave home late Friday afternoon in order to reach their destination in time for an early start Saturday morning. Some of them take the full week-end in the field and drive home early Monday, thus seeing another dawn, and missing Sunday evening traffic.

Within 50 or 100 miles of any city there are dozens of good places for birds. The enthusiast can readily make plans for so many different trips that it will take him years to go on all of them. Many birders, however, prefer to visit the same good birding areas repeatedly.

Your local bird club will know the best places for bird trips near you. Books have been written on the best places to see birds farther afield (see pp. 118-119).

Trips in Different Seasons

The presumed abundance, or presence, of certain birds, not the temperature or weather, should determine where and when to go on a bird trip. Birders go birding right through the year. In winter, even in the north, there are ducks and water birds to be seen. Spring migrants come pouring through from February to June.

Summer woods and fields are full of birds singing and nesting. In July the great southward shorebird migration begins. Land birds start moving in August. The fall migration is at its peak in September and October. Ducks and water birds that spend the summers in the far north are back on their winter grounds by November.

Each season has its own special attraction. In developing your bird trip plans, you should decide what trip is best suited for each particular time of year. A suggested calendar is given here. You can adapt this for your area by substituting the names of local places for the type of habitat. Your local bird club can help. Birders in the interior should substitute lakes, rivers, and reservoirs for the seashore and ocean.

The calendar is designed for the latitude of New York, Chicago, and northern California. Birders to the south will look for spring migrants from a week to a month earlier; for fall migrants, a week to a month later. Birders to the north will look

White pelicans occupy these nesting grounds at Pyramid Lake in Nevada. These large white birds also nest on islands in Great Salt Lake in Utah and in other parts of the Northwest.
Cy La Tour

BIRD TRIP CALENDAR

Week   *January*

1 Your area—Christmas census
2 Ocean—winter pelagic trip
3 All bodies of water—duck census
4 Waterfowl refuge—wintering ducks

February

1 Woods and bottomlands—wintering
  land birds
2 Open country—winter finches
3 Seashore—winter water birds
4 Woods and groves—owl roosts, nests

March

1 Land areas—early migrants
2 Waterfowl refuge—ducks, geese
3 Inland lakes and reservoirs—water birds
4 Edges and marshes—spring migrants
5 Woods and uplands—spring migrants

April

1 Waterfowl refuge—ducks, geese
2 Edges and marshes—spring migrants
3 Land areas—spring migrants
4 Land areas—spring migrants

May

1 Land areas—spring migrants
2 Land areas—warblers
3 Your area—Big Day
4 Your area—Round-up, or Campus Count
  (see p. 56 and p. 64)
5 Sand and mud flats—shorebirds

June

1 Sand and mud flats—shorebirds
2 Your area—breeding bird census, lowlands
3 Your area—breeding bird census, uplands
4 Mountain trip—breeding birds

July

1 Mountain trip—breeding birds
2 Ocean—pelagic trip
3 Sand and mud flats—shorebirds
4 Some new place—vacation trip

August

1 Some new place—vacation trip
2 Sand and mud flats—shorebirds
3 Sand and mud flats—shorebirds
4 Ocean—pelagic trip

September

1 Sand and mud flats—shorebirds
2 Mountain ridges—migrating hawks
3 Edges and uplands—fall land birds
4 Peninsulas and flyways—migrants
5 Peninsulas and flyways—migrants

October

1 Peninsulas and flyways—migrants
2 Mountain ridges—migrating hawks
3 Seashore—late migrants
4 Waterfowl refuge—ducks, geese
5 Lakes and reservoirs—early ducks

November

1 Land areas—winter visitors
2 Mountain ridges—last hawks
3 Waterfowl refuge—ducks, geese
4 Seashore—winter water birds

December

1 Lakes, reservoirs—wintering ducks
2 Waterfowl refuge—ducks, geese
3 Seashore—winter water birds
4 Your area—Christmas census

White-tailed ptarmigan, shown in summer plumage, is a bird of the high Rockies.

Edward Prins

Bird watchers here are "chumming" or putting out a line of food behind a boat on a pelagic trip. The food attracts various species of ocean birds for close viewing.

for spring migrants from one to three weeks later; fall migrants, from one to three weeks earlier. The trips suggested on the calendar need not be followed rigidly. The order of the different ones within any one month may often be varied to advantage.

Special Trips

Pelagic trip: This is an ocean or Gulf trip far enough out to sea to find such oceanic species as shearwaters, petrels, albatrosses, and jaegers.

You can sometimes see some of these from a party fishing boat, coastal vessel, or long-distance ferry. You will see more, however, if a group of bird watchers charters its own boat. Then you can stay as long as you want where birds are plentiful. You can also "chum up," or attract

the birds by baiting. Any oily bait will do—chopped-up fish livers are good; so is puffed wheat soaked in halibut oil, or suet chopped into ¼-inch squares. Bring an ample supply: a gallon of halibut oil, 2 boxes of puffed wheat, 20 pounds of suet, or even twice that much.

When you reach a likely territory offshore, start putting out this bait. Soon one or two birds will fly to your chum line. This will attract others, and you may get a large number close at hand where you can study them.

Mountain trip: As far as different types of plants and animals are concerned, going a thousand feet up a mountain is like going 300 miles north. A thousand feet may also equal a week's delay in the season.

The higher up you go the later is the season when birds start breeding

and keep on singing. Thus you can prolong your study of singing and breeding land birds by planning mountain trips on into June or July. Furthermore, at high altitudes you may find species, such as rosy finches and ptarmigan, that are rarely, if ever, found in the lowlands at the same latitude.

Vacation trip: As a dyed-in-the-wool birder, you may make your vacation trip a bird trip. You may go to the Gaspé Peninsula, to the Everglades, to Alaska, or to Mexico, to get new birds for your life list.

You may take your vacation in the spring, fall, or winter, in order to go during the right season to the places you want to visit. You may go to Rockport, Texas, a stopover for an impressive number of migrants in spring, or take a Caribbean trip in winter to add West Indian bird species to your life list.

Audubon Camp: The National Audubon Society operates adult summer camps for the study of natural history in Connecticut, Maine, Wisconsin, and California. Some state Audubon societies have camps for children as well as adults. Frequently these camps have two-week sessions. Spending your vacation at such a

The gannet colony on Bonaventure Island, at the mouth of the St. Lawrence River, is the largest colony of these birds found in North America. After the summer nesting season, these birds fly south and spend the winter along the Atlantic coast.

camp is an unusually good way to learn about birds and natural history.

August shorebird trip: In August, plan an all-day trip to the seashore where there are sand or mud flats. Good places are Monomoy, Massachusetts; Holgate (near Beach Haven), New Jersey; Port Bolivar (near Galveston), Texas; and Newport Beach (near Los Angeles), California. The southbound shorebird flight is more leisurely and protracted than the northward migration. You should see many birds on almost any day, but if you should happen to be there during a peak flight, it will be a memorable experience.

Waterfowl refuge: Waterfowl, when migrating or wintering, congregate in immense numbers at such refuges. The great flocks make magnificent spectacles either on the water or in the air.

Peninsulas: In the fall migration, enormous numbers of land birds regularly collect on certain peninsulas waiting for suitable wind and weather conditions before attempting to fly across the water to the south. Bird watchers, at such times, will see hundreds of birds of the same species in a matter of minutes. Flocks of small birds will be flying around. Thrushes will be calling endlessly overhead at night, keeping in touch with each other in the darkness.

At the very tip of land, bird after bird and species after species mount into the air and launch out southward over the water. Examples of such peninsulas are Cape May, New Jersey; Cape Charles, Virginia; and Point Pelee, Ontario.

Find out from maps or from experienced birders the points in your region where such migrants collect. Plan a fall visit there.

Mountain ridges: Many hawks migrate along north-south mountain ridges; or along ridges that go from northeast to southwest, or from northwest to southeast. When a strong wind from the west, for example, strikes such a ridge, the air is forced upward. On this updraft a hawk can coast southward for miles without once beating a wing.

Days with strong winds blowing at an angle to the ridge will thus bring impressive hawk flights. Watchers, collected at vantage points along these ridges, can identify and count these migrating hawks. Ducks, loons, jays, and other land birds often migrate along these ridges too.

Camp-outs and Club Week-ends

Some state Audubon societies schedule camp-outs or special bird week-ends each year. Places selected include, in season, such top bird concentration spots as Chatham, Massachusetts, and Cape May, New Jersey.

Going on such a week-end is fun and is an excellent way to learn about birds. Veteran birders are always on hand, anxious to help beginners. Organized field trips under experienced leaders should enable you to see many new species.

You will learn short-cuts in identification from good teachers and much about the habitat, habits, and history of the birds. Your local bird club should be able to obtain details about such scheduled bird week-ends.

Rockport, Texas, is famous for the great numbers of birds seen there during migration. Some cross the Gulf of Mexico; some follow the coast line, but they all seem to like Rockport.
George Prins

Listing the birds you see on a trip is sport, not science, but almost every bird watcher enjoys making such lists.

THE SPORT
OF BIRD
WATCHING

Bird watchers can have a great deal of fun with their hobby. Such fun is really sport, not science, though some who start bird watching as a pastime do end up by doing valuable ornithological work. Much of the sport involves making lists and seeing rare birds. Success depends upon the bird watcher's knowledge of bird habits and habitats, and his ability to identify birds.

Big Day

The biggest sporting event in the bird watcher's year is the Big Day. This is an attempt to see how many different species of birds one group can record in 24 hours. The Big Day

53

In many places the brown-headed cowbird would be a "common" bird for a Big Day list.

takes place at the height of the spring migration. Participants must be skilled at recognizing species.

The day starts long before dawn. The trip includes as many different habitats as possible. Each habitat has a list of "must" species — birds that can be found only in that habitat. The tight schedule allows only a limited time for each area. When all the "must" species from any one habitat have been spotted and listed, or when the time is up, the party is off to the next habitat.

"Common" birds will be seen along the way without special effort. "Bonus" birds are species that might be seen but that cannot be counted on and should not be specially looked for. Cumulative score cards, one for each habitat, show the "must," "common," and "bonus" species. These are checked off as seen, to help members of the party know how they stand during the day.

The people who plan the Big Day trip try to work out the most productive route for seeing birds. They try to locate unusual species in advance and then hope these birds will still be there on the Big Day. Local guides sometimes join the party to point out any special birds in their particular area.

The party usually starts out with some pre-dawn owl calling to get as many owls as possible on the list, and then listens for marsh birds at daybreak. In the early morning the party may cover low, marshy areas for land birds. Upland land birds are usually sought before noon.

In the afternoon the party often covers the seashore or lake shore, including marsh, bay, mud flat, and beach areas. Dusk is reserved for goatsuckers, more owls, and other night-singing birds.

During the day, meals and coffee are gulped in the car while en route. A list-checking dinner around eight o'clock winds up the trip, unless some night birds, missed before dawn, can still be located before midnight.

A party may drive two or three hundred miles in the course of a Big Day, and pile up an impressive total of birds seen. One party in New Jersey in 1959 recorded 180 species.

Here are the usual ground rules for a Big Day:

1. *Participants:* Any number.
2. *Area:* No limit.
3. *Transportation:* Any method.
4. *Time:* 24 hours, midnight to midnight.
5. *Purpose:* To record as many species of birds as possible on a combined party list. Participants may also keep individual lists.
6. *What counts:* Any living, wild species of bird seen or heard by a competent observer with the party. Dead, captive, wing-clipped, or domestic species do not count; nor does an egg.

7. *Party:* Participants must stay together. Species will be counted only when recorded by members of the party who are within sight of each other when in a car, or within hearing of each other (or not separated from the main party for more than 15 minutes) when on foot.
8. *Species:* Only full species as recognized by the latest *A.O.U. Checklist* count. A species is only counted once, irrespective of the number of sub-species observed.
9. *Identification by family or genus:* Will count if no other members of the same family or genus are counted (e.g. hummingbird, *Buteo*, *Empidonax*). Hybrids count only if neither parent is recorded.
10. *Observations:* Will count if made by any competent observer familiar with the species. Rare or unfamiliar birds must be observed by two participants. If in doubt—leave it out.

Big Morning

A Big Morning is like a Big Day, but it ends at noon and thus takes up less time and energy. Many persons can spend a morning bird watching, but not a whole day. The route must be planned to include as many habitats as possible in half the time. Participants have sometimes been

On a Small Day, birdwatchers concentrate on observing bird behavior in the field. This plover is apparently trying to distract attention from its nest.

Edward Prins

able to record a list 75 per cent as large as that of a Big Day.

The Big Day and Big Morning can be carried out on a state, county, peninsula, or other area basis. A person may, of course, go on a Big Day alone, but a group of eight to twelve persons in three cars makes an ideal party.

Small Day

Some bird watchers prefer a Small Day to a Big Day. The purpose of a Small Day is to see a few birds at length, rather than to see many birds briefly. Select a good quiet bird haunt away from traffic, and investigate it at your leisure. Take one hour or ten. Start at dawn or high noon. Go alone or with one or two friends.

Study the birds you see. Follow them with your eyes, ears, or glasses for a long period. See what they are doing. Watch their behavior. Learn their songs. Make yourself part of their world. This is the best way to learn about birds.

Round-up

Round-ups usually take place in the spring and fall, though they can be held at any time. A Round-up is the sport of listing all the species of birds

Canada geese often mate for life. The female incubates the eggs but the gander stands guard nearby during the breeding season.

that can be seen in one day or one week-end in a given region, such as the State of Massachusetts, the Delaware Valley, Chicago and its environs, or Los Angeles County. As many parties as wish may participate.

Most Round-ups differ from a Christmas or other census by including more territory and by emphasizing the number of species rather than the exact count of all individual birds. However, some localities conduct Spring Round-ups in exactly the same manner as their Christmas

counts (15-mile circle, species and number of individuals, etc.).

Rare Bird Alert (RBA)

If you want to see rare birds, organize or join a Rare Bird Alert in your area. This is a group of bird watchers who telephone each other, in a prescribed order, whenever any member sees a rare bird. It is the duty of each member to call immediately the next person on the list as soon as he sees or is notified about the pres-ence of a rare bird within the area.

Each caller passes on information as to where the bird was seen, when, and by whom, and any other significant details of behavior or identification. The list of members and telephone numbers should be kept next to the telephone, since an RBA call must be passed on at once!

Groups of beginners, advanced bird watchers, or experts can have their own rare bird alert. They merely need a prior understanding as to which species they will regard as rare.

Helen Cruickshank—National Audubon Society

The little green heron is one of the most common herons of the eastern United States.

BIRD LISTS

The Trip List

Almost every bird watcher keeps lists of the birds he sees. The simplest is perhaps the trip list—that is, the birds noted on any one trip. Species are usually checked off on a field card (p. 18) as they are seen. Since identification by sound can be as accurate as identification by sight, birds are counted whether seen or heard. But species heard only are properly marked "(H)."

In addition to the names of the species observed, the trip list may also include: date, time in field, route, wind, weather, temperature, and the names of the observers. The total count or estimate of the numbers of individual birds of each species is also recorded.

Each person on the trip may keep his own individual list, but a composite list for the whole party will be made, too. The leader makes this list at the end of the trip, perhaps during dinner. He calls aloud the name of each species on the field card. If you have seen a particular species, you will tell the leader the number of individuals you saw. So will all the other members. The leader adds these all together and tries to eliminate obvious duplications.

If a trip is to last several days, you may want to keep one list for each day, or a list for each resort or national park visited, as well as a composite list for the entire vacation.

If you are a "habitat hound," you may, even on a day's trip, keep a list for each habitat visited, and then combine them into one joint list.

The Year List

Many bird watchers keep a year list, or a list with dates and places of every species of bird seen during the year from January 1 through December 31. These lists can be compared from year to year. You may find it amusing to see if this year's list will be larger than last year's or larger than that of some fellow bird watcher.

Some enthusiasts keep a spring list and a fall list, with special emphasis on the arrival and departure of migrants, including dates first and last seen. Further information may include the date the bird was first heard singing, and dates of first nest, eggs, or young. Lists can be fun, and if the records you keep are accurate, they may also be a useful addition to the ornithological data of your area.

The Life List

The life list is one that almost every bird watcher keeps. You will probably want to keep one too. It is a record of each different species of bird you see for the first time during

your life, with date and place seen. There are 686 species of birds that occur annually in North America north of Mexico. It is doubtful if any one person has ever seen all 686, but it might be possible over many years to see most of them if the nearly extinct birds, the short-tailed albatross, Eskimo curlew, and ivory-billed woodpecker, were excluded.

If you travel to Mexico, the West Indies, Europe, or anywhere else in the world, you can put many new species on your life list. If you visit the tropics, you could list hundreds more, provided that you could identify them. Owing in part to the greater diversity of habitat, the tropics have many more species than the temperate zones.

Scientists have named about 8,600 species of birds. To see each of these in the wild in one lifetime would be impossible. Ludlow Griscom, the champion field observer of our time, probably had the world's largest life list—over 3,000 species. Stricken, but indomitable, he added 400 species to this list while on a wheel-chair safari in Africa in 1958, the year before he died. Most of us, however, will be

Trip lists are the simplest lists kept by bird watchers.

BIRD WATCHERS' DAILY CHECK LIST

Observers Chelsea Bird Club
Date 9/17/60 Locality Cape May
Weather Fair Total 62
Add'l Species None

		Hawk, Sparrow	
Loon, Common		Grouse, Ruffed	
Loon, Red-throated		Bobwhite	
Grebe, Red-necked		Pheasant, Ring-necked	
Grebe, Horned		Turkey	
Grebe, Pied-billed		Rail, King	
Petrel, Wilson's		Rail, Clapper	✓
		Rail, Virginia	

content with a life list of a few hundred species.

Part of the fun of bird watching is putting new birds on your life list. Any trip that adds a "new life," as the phrase goes, is a red-letter occasion. If you have identified the bird by yourself, you will feel special satisfaction.

The Property List

Homeowners and home renters often keep a list of the birds seen on their property. This can be kept by the year, by the season (spring and fall migration), or for the entire time you live on that property.

Species are generally counted on such a list if they are *seen* or *heard* *on* or *from* the property. This permits you to include birds flying across the sky or singing from your neighbor's apple tree.

People who live in apartments sometimes keep lists of the birds they see from their windows. Shut-ins often do, too. Some city dwellers have only a straggling ailanthus tree and a few strands of ivy in a tiny backyard. But they build up, over the years, a remarkable list of migrants that have dropped down to their tiny oases of green. This may even include such wild woods birds as the hermit thrush and ovenbird.

BIRD CENSUSES

Most bird watchers get their first chance to make a contribution to science by taking part in a bird census. For bird watchers, the chief census is probably the annual Christmas Bird Count, organized and operated by the National Audubon Society in conjunction with the United States Fish and Wildlife Service.

The Christmas Count

This count was started in 1900 by the famous ornithologist Frank M. Chapman as a substitute for the "Christmas hunt," then a favorite

holiday pastime. The popularity of this Christmas census has greatly exceeded early expectations. From 27 persons and 25 reports the first year, it had grown by 1959 to include about 8,000 observers in 594 parties, operating in virtually every state and province in North America north of Mexico.

The immediate purpose of the Christmas census is to count every bird to be found within a given area on one day within a period of about ten days that includes Christmas and New Year's.

To make this count significant, rigid ground rules apply. The area should fill, but must not exceed, a diameter of fifteen miles. At least eight hours must be spent in the field, except in the Arctic or at sea. Data must be submitted on temperature, wind, weather, route, and types and relative amounts of habitat covered. This, plus the names of the species seen, the numbers of individuals of each, and the names of participants, are published annually in a Christmas Bird Count issue of *Audubon Field Notes.*

In some areas as many as 40 or 50

Brown pelicans and ducks can be seen off the coast of Florida. Because so many birds winter there, Florida always has a record Christmas Count. In 1960, 200 species were counted by one group of observers.

A breeding bird census west of the Rockies might include a nesting magpie.

persons now participate in the count. The entire area is divided into sectors. Teams of from two to four persons are assigned to each sector and comb it thoroughly.

In coastal areas one team may be sent out to sea. Other team members watch for birds from rock piles jutting into the ocean. One or two groups in boats check the bird population in creeks, bays, and inland waterways. Other teams cover the various land sectors.

Observers are in the field before dawn and do not stop till after sundown. Even lunch is eaten at a spot convenient for watching birds.

In the evening the various teams assemble at a restaurant for dinner. Afterward, the area leader reads down the list of species. Each team captain calls out the numbers of each species observed in his sector. Thus the final list is made up.

Counts vary with the region. A record of 200 species was obtained in 1960 by observers at Cocoa, Florida. Thirteen participants, however, at Arvida, Quebec, with the temperature from 9° to 26° below zero, were not displeased one year with a total of only 12 species after eight hours in the field in 15 inches of snow.

The scientific results of the Christmas Count have been noteworthy. An increasingly comprehensive and usable amount of bird population data has been accumulated over more than sixty years. This permits scientists to study bird population trends and their relation to changes in habitat, weather, climate, and man's changes in the environment. First evidence of significant regional or nation-wide decreases, or increases, in numbers of a species are often revealed by the Christmas Count, as are also extensions or contractions of range.

The Waterfowl Census

Censuses of wintering waterfowl are made on one or more days in mid-winter after the close of the hunting season. Census takers cover every body of water or watercourse in their area to count ducks, geese, and swans. Sometimes helicopters and cameras are used to record the vast concentra-tions in certain Southern sounds and sanctuaries. Federal wildlife officials take such counts every year. They are sometimes assisted by members of local bird clubs.

The Hawk Watch

The autumnal hawk watch is a recent development in bird watching. On a designated day in September and on another in October, members of participating bird clubs man lookout posts on the ridges on the main hawk flyways. They keep a record of the different kinds and numbers of hawks observed migrating along the ridges that day. With observers in several states participating at various

A breeding bird census in the Southeast might include the painted bunting. On a Christmas Count it would probably appear only in southern Florida or along the Gulf Coast.

Helen Cruickshank—National Audubon Society

vantage points, it is becoming possible to obtain basic information on the numbers and population trends of hawks. Such data, adjusted for weather conditions, become of increasing value as they accumulate over the years.

The Breeding Bird Census

The most complicated census, perhaps, is the annual census of breeding birds. A chosen area, the same each year, is accurately described as to kinds and amounts of habitats. The census, taken throughout the breeding season, ascertains, among other things, the species present and the numbers of breeding pairs and nonbreeding individuals. The National Audubon Society publishes these results in its *Audubon Field Notes*.

Participation in a breeding bird census involves intensive application and persistence. It is not to be undertaken lightly, but is a most rewarding experience. If you think you might be interested in making scientific investigations of birds, this is a good way to start.

Your local bird club should be able to find out about these various censuses and to tell you which ones you may be able to participate in.

A Campus Bird Count

Bird watchers at certain schools and colleges hold an annual Campus Bird Count, usually in early May. Only the area owned by the institution is included. Since this area remains the same from year to year, comparable figures on spring population trends can be accumulated.

In cold climates participants in the Christmas Census may be rewarded with seeing only a few species of wintering birds in their area.

John H. Gerard—National Audubon Society

Female and male rose-breasted grosbeaks are among the many species of North American birds that have been known to respond to artificial feeding.

ATTRACTING BIRDS ABOUT YOUR HOME

The beauty and songs of birds add much to the pleasures of home and garden. Birds are responsive creatures. By providing food, water, and shelter, you can attract them to your house and grounds.

Seventy or more species in North America regularly respond to artificial feeding. Chief among these are hummingbirds; woodpeckers and jays; chickadees, nuthatches, and creepers; robins, catbirds, and thrashers; blackbirds, cowbirds, grackles, and orioles; sparrows, grosbeaks, buntings, and finches; and starlings and house sparrows.

Ducks, geese, and coots will come for food thrown on the ground, as will doves, pigeons, quail, and pheas-

ant. So will gulls, who are scavengers and are on the lookout for handouts.

Food may, of course, be just tossed on the ground or in water. Indeed, gulls, ducks, and chicken-like birds will accept it only that way. It should be remembered, though, that ground feeding makes birds particularly vulnerable to cats. But smaller birds will also come to a feeding tray, bird table, feeding stick, or suet holder.

Feeding Trays

A feeding tray outside the kitchen, dining room, or bedroom will entice birds to your window. Later, if you leave the window open, they may come inside, and even onto your

from Fish and Wildlife Service. U.S. Dept. of the Interior

hand or shoulder, if you have the patience to train them to do so.

Various types of feeders are on the market, or you can build one yourself. The simplest, perhaps, is a shelf nailed onto the sill just outside the window. To feed the birds, just open the window and put the food out on the shelf.

Another simple feeder is a "bird table," about 2 by 3 feet, set on a post about 4 or 5 feet high. Put it at least 10 feet away from the nearest fence or branch, so that squirrels or cats cannot conveniently jump onto it.

A more elaborate tray or table may have a self-feeding bin in the center, or on the side. It may also be covered to protect it from the weather. A tray equipped with weather vanes and set on a pole will swing in the wind and will protect the feeding birds from wintry blasts.

A feeder should have a few holes in the floor to draw off rain or melting snow. A raised border will serve as a perch and will keep food from being blown or scattered off the tray. The supporting pole should be protected by a sloping collar against cats and squirrels (see picture on p. 72).

Natural perches and nearby cover are desirable. For your own enjoyment put feeders where you can see them from your dining room, kitchen, or living-room windows.

Other Feeding Devices

Chickadees and nuthatches like to eat at a "chickadee-diner." This is a flat or round board, or a cut branch. It should be about one foot long, and should have a number of one-inch holes bored into it with a bit. Nail it to the window sill like a feeding tray. The holes are filled with suet, seeds, or peanut butter mixed with gravel.

Evening grosbeaks use a "self-feeding" type of feeder.

Hal H. Harrison—National Audubon Society

The hummingbird is getting sugar water from a special hummingbird feeder.

If tacked up vertically on a tree or suspended from a branch or wire, it is sometimes called a "feeding stick."

Chickadees will also cling to a round seed-studded ball of suet that is hung from a branch or wire. Tree-climbing birds, such as woodpeckers, chickadees, nuthatches, and creepers, will come to suet nailed to a tree trunk. A more efficient way is to put the suet in small-mesh cloth netting. This will keep it from being torn off the nail by a starling, or falling to the ground. A note of warning: during cold weather, birds may hurt their eyes on metal suet containers.

The simplest form of humming-bird feeder is a tilted test tube filled with sugar water (two parts water to one part sugar). Suspend the tube by a wire outside a window or porch, or from an arbor in the garden. A more elaborate arrangement is a revolving, double-decked, circular stand with from 6 to 24 test tubes and perches. The test tubes may have openings with borders that simulate red flowers—varieties that are much favored by hummingbirds.

Food for Birds

Birds that come to feeders will respond to a variety of foods. Many of the winter birds are seed eaters. Cardinals and other grosbeaks are especially fond of sunflower seeds. Most birds like bread crumbs, peanut butter, raisins, and suet. Some like peanuts, crushed walnuts or pecans, and oatmeal.

Seeds for wild birds can be bought in bags (weighing 5 to 100 pounds) at grocery stores, hardware stores, and supermarkets. Such mixtures usually include buckwheat, cracked corn, seeds of hemp and millet, and sunflower seeds.

A "bird cafeteria" will help you find out the kinds of seed the birds in your area like best. Divide your feeding table into six or eight compartments with strips of wood. Put an equal amount of a different kind of seed in each compartment. See which kinds are eaten first.

Ducks, geese, and chicken-like birds will take cracked corn and other poultry mixtures. Gulls will eat stale bread or scraps of almost any food.

Keep your feeders clean at all times. Birds can get diseases from moldy food.

It has been said that a bird's teeth are in its stomach. These "teeth" are actually bits of grit in its gizzard that help digest its food. That is why doves and pigeons often pick up gravel along the roadside.

You can also supply grit at your feeder. Fill a small box or compartment on the feeder with coarse sand, gravel, and crushed oyster or egg shells. Shells are especially valuable to female birds during the spring, when they need calcium to build up the shells of their own eggs.

Keeping Up the Service

If you feed in winter, it is important to keep it up throughout the entire season. This would be from early October to late April in the latitude of New York or Chicago. You can start earlier and stop later farther north; start later and stop earlier farther south. But don't stop winter feeding once you have started! Your

Don't start feeding birds in winter unless you keep it up. Otherwise the birds may starve.
AMNH

Hal H. Harrison—National Audubon Society

Chickadees like a feeder which holds both suet and seeds.

birds may perish because they may have become dependent upon you for food. If you have to leave home for a few days, try to set up an automatic feeder that will keep the birds supplied with food while you are gone; or arrange to have a neighbor come over to fill your feeders.

Although it is important to continue feeding once you have started, it is equally important that the birds should not be entirely dependent on your feeder for their sustenance. So unless there is an emergency, like deep snow, ice storms, or extreme cold, don't let the birds in your neighborhood depend entirely on you—let them forage elsewhere sometimes for themselves.

Many persons put out food for birds all year round. Summer or winter, birds will always be attracted by a supply of edibles. In summer, robins, catbirds, mockingbirds, and others like such fruit as grapes, oranges, sliced apples, and bananas. But these and other species will also take the same kinds of food in summer as they do in winter.

How Many Feeders, and Where?

For a small yard you need only a window tray, a bird table, a feeding stick, and a suet holder. In fact, birds will come to any single one of these. But if you have a larger yard you may put up a few more.

Birds do not usually come to a feeder on an upper floor unless they are led to it. This can be done by getting the birds accustomed to coming to a feeder on a lower floor. Then put the feeder on a trolley or hoist. Move it a little each day until it is outside an upper window. If the daily move is not too great, the birds will continue to come to feed.

Bird feeders need not be elaborate to attract birds. It is more important that they be put in a place where the birds using them will be safe from predators.
AMNH

Since tree swallows nest in holes in trees, they will also nest in bird houses.

BIRD HOUSES

Over thirty species of North American birds, many of which originally nested in holes in trees or in caves, will now build their nests in bird houses or other sites provided by man. Such species include the wood duck, sparrow hawk, screech owl, woodpecker, swallow, chickadee, titmouse, nuthatch, wren, and bluebird. House sparrows and starlings will often use houses put out for other species.

Entrances

To persuade a bird to use a bird house, pay particular attention to the size of the entrance hole and to the location of the house. You can buy bird houses at some hardware stores, at bird supply shops, or from birdhouse manufacturers, or you can build them yourself. If you buy one, specify the species it is supposed to house. Ask for a bluebird house, or a flicker house, or a wren house, *by name.* Each one has a hole of a size to keep out a larger bird.

When and Where to Put Up the House

Bird houses can be put up at any time. If put up late in summer, how-

TYPES OF BIRD HOUSES

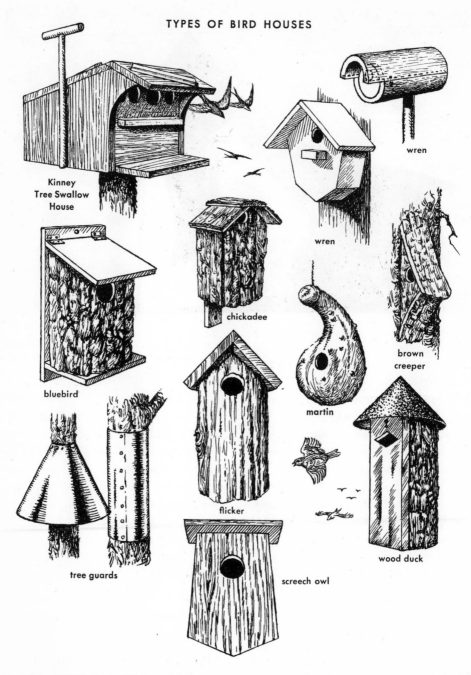

Kinney
Tree Swallow
House

wren

wren

chickadee

brown
creeper

bluebird

martin

flicker

tree guards

screech owl

wood duck

from Fish and Wildlife Service. U.S. Dept. of the Interior

ever, you can more easily determine which positions are shaded and which are not. Furthermore, over the winter the houses will have a chance to weather, which makes them more attractive to the birds.

The house, as a rule, should face south, or away from the prevailing storm winds in the area. It should be sheltered by a projecting roof so that rain can not come in the entrance hole. Screw the mounting board, on which the house is set, upright against a pole, tree trunk, or branch; or tilt it slightly forward (but never backward—that might let rain in). Natural perches nearby are a convenience to birds. Put the house in or near a habitat favored by the species for which it is designed.

Once a year clean out the old nest from the house, because it may contain parasites. Let the tenants build a fresh nest each spring. Fix bird houses, as you do feeders, so that predators can not get to them. You can rat-proof, cat-proof, and squirrel-proof a tree or pole by putting a broad, sloping metal collar on it. You can also secure the same protection by suspending the box from a branch with a wire.

How Many Houses?

During the breeding season, a pair of birds of one species will establish territorial rights to a certain piece of ground, and will drive away other members of the same species. Hence, in a small yard, it is useless to put up more than one house for each species. Birds of different species, however, do not mind being fairly close together. Their houses can be placed within 25 feet of each other. And a few birds—tree swallows, for example—are so sociable that they will not compete with any other birds, not even those of the same species. Several of their houses can be set up in close proximity.

Apartments for Martins

Purple martins are our only birds that will nest in bird apartment houses. Consequently, martin houses usually have from 8 to 16 compartments. But they can have more. They are somewhat complicated to make. If you buy one, prices range from $20 to $50.

Place the house on a 15- to 20-foot pole sunk securely in the ground. Put

A house for purple martins.
W. T. Davidson—National Audubon Society

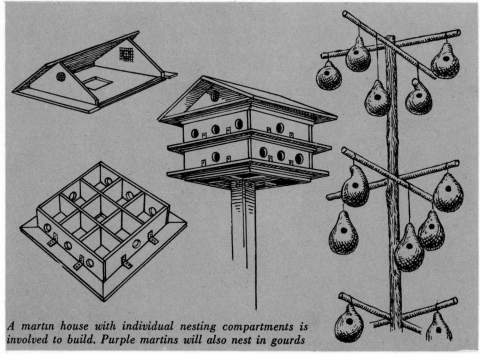

A martin house with individual nesting compartments is involved to build. Purple martins will also nest in gourds

from Fish and Wildlife Service. U.S. Dept. of the Interior

it out in the open and not too near your house. Martins can be quite noisy.

Martins will also nest in hollowed-out gourds. Bottle gourds or other hard-shelled varieties are the most suitable. Several of these may be hung on cross bars on a pole set into the ground. Gourd-nesting martin colonies are more often seen in the South than in the North.

The Kinney Tree Swallow House

The special features of this house are the three 1-inch feeding holes in addition to the 1½-inch entrance hole. These smaller holes permit more rapid feeding of the young because the parents do not have to enter the house in order to feed them. The parents thus spend more time on the wing insect-hunting; and this helps the young to survive in bad weather when insects are scarce.

This type of house also has a perch in the shape of a "T" nailed to the outside of one of its walls. It enables the male to stand guard during the time when the female is incubating the eggs. There are also cleats on the roof which provide a toe-hold for the birds.

Special Housing Needs

The following species have special requirements for their nesting houses:

Barn owl: Nail a small barrel (about 18 inches deep and approximately 10 inches in diameter) lengthwise, with one end open or half open, on a branch or in a crotch of a tree, 12 to 18 feet high.

Flicker: Fill the house with sawdust and shavings to a depth of 2 inches.

Woodpeckers, chickadees, titmice, nuthatches: These species prefer unfinished, roofed houses made of slabs of wood. If bark-covered wood is not available, weathered lumber will do. Because these birds prefer to nest in the woods, they will use bird houses set up in a shady place.

House wren: Put up several roofed houses. The polygamous male will make a dummy nest in each. Few will go to waste, as he sometimes has two or more mates. The entrance hole for the house wren and for *Bewick's wren* should be a vertical slot about 1¼ inches high by 3 inches wide, so that the birds can bring in the long twigs they prefer for constructing the foundation of the nest. The correct size of the vertical slot for the *Carolina wren* box is 1½ inches high by 3 inches wide—it houses a slightly larger bird. Durable wren houses also can be made of coconuts. One birder set up such a house in New Haven which lasted for 30 years and was always occupied.

The Roosting Box

Certain species of birds that nest in houses will often roost in the same houses after the nesting season is over, particularly in winter and bad weather.

Specially made roosting boxes with staggered perches will house more individual birds than will nesting houses. So, if you want to keep more birds about your home in winter, put up special roosting boxes in the fall. Build such a box in accordance with the specifications on page 77, but include six or eight perches, ¼ inch in diameter. These should be glued into shallow holes that have been drilled in the inside walls.

from Fish and Wildlife Service. U.S. Dept. of the Interior

Roosting boxes are of great value to birds during cold weather. They are built like bird houses but have a number of interior perches added. The perches should not be directly over each other. Roosting boxes should face south and be in a protected area.

CERTAIN PREFERRED LOCATIONS

Wood duck: lowland timber not far from water

Sparrow hawk: trees by edge of woods and open fields

Screech owl: apple orchard

Great crested flycatcher: open woodland, pastures, and orchards

Chickadee, titmouse, nuthatch: old orchards and woodland borders

Bluebird: open, sunlit orchard

Carolina wren: woodland borders and brushy areas

Tree swallow: near water

Song sparrow: thickets

House finch: orchards and dooryard shrubbery

Phoebe: near water (especially beneath bridges)

Flicker and red-headed woodpecker: directly above surrounding foliage

Downy and hairy woodpecker: orchard and open woodland

Saw-whet owl: open grove

Barn owl: large trees

SPECIFICATIONS FOR NESTING SHELVES

Species	Size of Floor (in.)	Depth of House (in.)	Height above Ground (ft.)
Robin	6x8	8	6-15
Barn swallow	6x6	6	8-12
Song sparrow	6x6	6	1-3
Phoebe	6x6	6	8-12

—from Fish and Wildlife Service
U.S. Dept. of the Interior

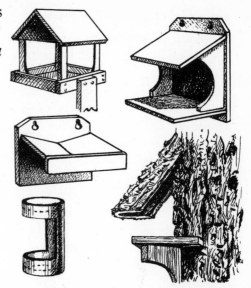

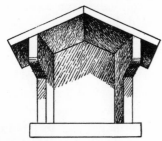

Nesting shelves will be accepted by several species of birds that normally nest in the open and that will not, therefore, use bird houses.

SPECIFICATIONS FOR BIRD HOUSES

Species	Size of Floor (in.)	Depth of House (in.)	Height of Hole Above Floor (in.)	Diameter of Hole (in.)	Height Above Ground (ft.)
Bluebird	5x5	8	6	1½	5-10
Chickadee	4x4	8-10	6-8	1⅛	6-15
Titmouse	4x4	8-10	6-8	1¼	6-15
Nuthatch	4x4	8-10	6-8	1¼	12-20
House wren & Bewick's wren	4x4	6-8	4-6	1-1¼	6-10
Carolina wren	4x4	6-8	4-6	1½	6-10
Violet-green swallow & tree swallow	5x5	6	1-5	1½	10-15
Purple martin*	6x6	6	1	2½	15-20
House finch	6x6	6	4	2	8-12
Starling	6x6	16-18	14-16	2	10-25
Great crested flycatcher	6x6	8-10	6-8	2	8-20
Flicker	7x7	16-18	14-16	2½	6-20
Red-headed woodpecker	6x6	12-15	9-12	2	12-20
Downy woodpecker	4x4	8-10	6-8	1¼	6-20
Hairy woodpecker	6x6	12-15	9-12	1½	12-20
Screech owl	8x8	12-15	9-12	3	10-30
Saw-whet owl	6x6	10-12	8-10	2½	12-20
Barn owl	10x18	15-18	4	6	12-18
Sparrow hawk	8x8	12-15	9-12	3	10-30
Wood duck	10x18	10-24	12-16	4	10-20

*Per compartment.

Other Artificial Sites

Some species, such as phoebes and robins, can be attracted by boards, beams, joists, and shelves placed either horizontally or vertically. Nesting shelves can be bought; or a simple one in the form of a flat board can be put up with a bracket.

The barn swallow builds its mud nests inside barns, on or against beams and joists. A window or door in your barn should be kept open all summer, so the swallows can fly back and forth.

The cliff swallow builds its mud nests outside barns, under the eaves. If the walls of your barn are too smooth, nail under the eaves a row of rough planks to which the birds can attach their mud nests. If these nests are knocked down (in the late fall), they will not be taken over by house sparrows. The swallows will return each spring and construct new nests. Specifications for nesting shelves are given here. Select spots for these shelves on your porch or around your house or outbuildings where you can have the pleasure of watching the birds raise their families.

How to Make and Install Your Own Bird House

Avoid metal—it gets too hot in the sun. Use 3/4-inch or 1/2-inch seasoned lumber; cypress is the most durable. If possible, treat lumber with wood preservative before construction. Cut lumber to dimensions given on page 77, and assemble in accordance with drawings. Use brass screws or galvanized nails to join pieces together. Stain natural color after assembly; or paint brown, green, or gray.

Houses exposed to sun, such as martins' and tree swallows' houses, should be painted white to reflect heat.

The roof should slant forward, overhang, and be hinged so the house can be opened for yearly cleaning. Bore several 1/4-inch holes in the floor for drainage, and in front *above* the entrance hole for ventilation.

If you wish, screw the house on a mounting board 1 x 12 x 24 inches, and screw or nail the mounting board on a pole, tree trunk, or branch.

Encircle the trunk or pole with a sloping anti-predator collar.

If you wish to be able to take very brief looks inside a nest while it is in use, hinge a side wall. On that side install a pane of glass (set in grooves *within* the house) to protect the birds when the hinged wall is opened.

The table on page 77 gives house specifications for different species. Follow carefully the hole sizes indicated. If holes are too big, tenants will be ousted by larger birds; if too small, tenants of your choice cannot enter.

Plans for a simple type of bird house are given on the opposite page.

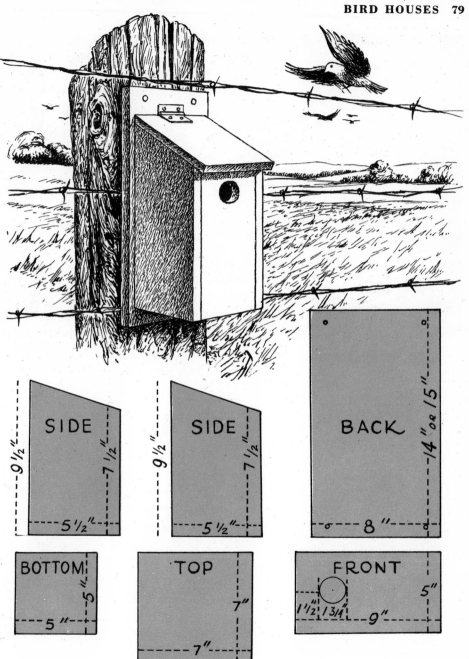

SIDE

9½"

7½"

5½"

SIDE

9½"

7½"

5½"

BACK

14" or 15"

8"

BOTTOM

5"

5"

TOP

7"

7"

FRONT

5"

1½" 13/4"

9"

A Bullock's oriole enjoys a bath. This type of bird bath is one of the easiest to build, but it gives the birds no protection from their enemies.

BIRD BATHS

Birds require water for bathing and drinking. Hence they will be attracted by a bird bath. This should be shallow, perhaps 3 inches deep in the middle, with sloping sides and a rough bottom surface. You can make one yourself with concrete. Or you can buy a ready-made bath from a ceramics or garden supply house.

Tips on Bird Baths

Be sure to place the bird bath in an area which gives some protection against cats. The bath should be ele-vated about 3 feet off the ground and placed near hanging branches of a tree. If it is in an open area, the birds have a better chance of seeing a prowling cat and of escaping.

In winter when streams are frozen, you can keep the water unfrozen in your bird bath by using a submersion heater. This can be thermostatically controlled. Attach the heater to an electric-light extension cord and plug it into an outlet in your house. The birds in your garden can then have warmed water even on the coldest days. Indeed, in very cold weather they may put their feet in the bath just to warm them up! Buy such a heater from a tropical fish store or a poultry supply house.

Birds prefer running water to stagnant, and a fountain is a special delight to them.

A bucket with a tiny hole in the bottom, suspended 2 or 3 feet over a bird bath, is an unusually effective way of attracting birds. They seem fascinated by the drip, drip, drip of the water through the tiny hole. Many species that you might not otherwise see will come to investigate it, particularly during migration. The bucket can be partially concealed by leaves for the sake of appearance. A wooden one lends a rustic touch.

The Dust Bath

Some birds like dust baths. Perhaps these help them get rid of external parasites, such as bird lice and ticks. (These parasites are harmless to man.) A bare spot of ground covered with loose earth will serve as a dust wallow. It is another means of drawing and keeping birds around your home, where you can watch and study them conveniently.

A drip-bucket is a simple and a very effective way of attracting birds to your yard. It is especially popular during migration seasons.

To encourage birds about your home, plan to leave part of your property in its natural state.

COVER FOR BIRDS

Providing cover is one of the most important ways, and one of the easiest, to attract birds. Cover includes thickets, bushes, brush piles, hedges, unkempt corners, piles of logs or debris, and briar patches. Birds can dive into these to escape from their enemies. They can hide and rest there. Remember how Bre'r Rabbit and Peter Rabbit loved the tangle of their briar patches? The security offered by a tangle is a powerful attraction to birds, too.

The Untidy, Attractive Yard

Deliberately plan to leave part of your property in its natural state. It will mean less work for you: less lawn to mow, fewer beds to weed, fewer trees to spray. Don't be forever raking and pruning and chopping.

Insects are attracted to a dead or dying tree. Birds are attracted by insects. Chickadees and titmice nest in holes in dead branches. Woodpeckers and owls nest in holes in dead trees.

Leave some dead branches and dead trees for them.

Do this and you will have many more birds than your neighbor who cleans up and burns all his brush, cuts away dead wood, and sprays all his trees.

Building Shelters

You can also make more cover. John Terres in his book (listed on page 118) tells how to construct a really good brush pile. In the fall select a site for this brush pile, perhaps in a corner of your property or in your vegetable garden. Or, put it right out in your backyard where you can see it from the kitchen or dining-room window.

Collect all the branches you can, large and small. Break them into 6- or 8-foot lengths. Lay the larger ones on the ground in a square with the ends crosswise on top of each other. Add branches on alternate sides till you have built the pile about 5 feet high. Then use smaller ones to taper the pile toward the top. Roof it over with twigs and evergreens. After Christmas, old Christmas trees will provide an extra supply of roofing.

You now have a wonderful shelter for small birds, where they are protected from their enemies (unless you have a neighborhood cat) and shielded somewhat from the wind, rain, sleet, and snow. If the shelter is not unsightly or in the way, leave it up all year. Or tear it down in spring, and pile the branches behind your garage till the next fall.

Your brush pile, however, does not have to be as elaborate as this. Even

Farmers often provide feeding and shelter areas for quail and pheasants.

if you just pile all your old branches together in one place, you will be giving the birds a useful shelter.

The Old Christmas Tree

After Christmas you may want to make a special Christmas-tree shelter for birds. Collect several old Christmas trees from your neighbors and pile them up in some inconspicuous place on your property. Tie them down so they cannot blow away. Evergreens with their branches piled in this way make an ideal and natural bird shelter—your Christmas present to the birds.

If you have sloping ground you can make a hillside shelter. Put a crossbar four feet up on a tree near the base of a slope. Nail the end of a long pole on each end of this crossbar, like shafts on a carriage. Support the other ends of these poles on the ground of the slope. Nail slats or tar paper across the top of the poles. Cover the shelter with evergreen boughs or other tree branches. Now the birds have a roof with three sides open. You can attract sparrows, doves, quail, and pheasants under such a shelter.

If you are ingenious, you can think up other kinds of bird shelters adapted to your property and to the materials you have on hand.

Brush piles, hillside shelters, and old Christmas trees will attract birds to your home during the winter because they provide a place for the birds to rest.

Edward Prins

Evergreens provide both food and shelter for many kinds of birds. Plan to have at least ten per cent of your plantings for your home in evergreens.

PLANTING TO ATTRACT BIRDS

You can attract many birds to your house and grounds by planting the kinds of trees, shrubs, and flowers that birds like for food, shelter, or nesting sites.

number of common birds. The United States Fish and Wildlife Service gathered this data over many years in order to determine the value of various species of birds to the farmer.

Planting for Food

For food, some birds prefer sunflower seeds or the hard seeds of conifers. Other birds prefer soft fruits such as cherries or mulberries. Still other birds eat the buds of trees or shrubs. In the tables that follow are listed the favorite plants of a

Planting for Shelter

For shelter, birds like evergreens, shrubs, hedges, or briars. Bushes or shrubs for nesting places should have many crotches and forks. Proper pruning will often encourage bushes to produce such crotches. Bushy borders of gardens or property lines

85

	Alders	Ashes	Aspens	Bayberries	Beeches	Birches	Blackberries	Black Gums	Blueberries	Buckthorns	Buffaloberry	Cedars	Cherries, Wild	Dogwoods	Elderberries	Elms	Firs	Gooseberries	Grapes, Wild	Greenbrier	Hackberry	Hawthorns	Hazels	Hemlocks
Bluebird				•			•		•			•	•	•	•							•		
Cardinal							•		•				•	•	•				•	•	•			
Catbird				•			•		•	•	•	•	•	•	•				•		•	•		
Chickadee				•	•				•								•	•						•
Crossbill												•					•							•
Duck, Wood		•			•												•		•					
Finch, Purple	•	•	•		•			•					•		•		•							
Flycatcher, Crested													•	•										
Goldfinch	•																•							
Grosbeak		•		•	•		•					•	•	•	•	•			•			•	•	
Jay				•	•		•		•				•		•				•					
Junco																								
Kingbird									•				•	•	•				•					
Mockingbird							•	•					•	•	•				•	•	•	•		
Nuthatch					•										•		•							
Oriole							•		•						•									
Phainopepla										•			•		•				•					
Phoebe							•		•						•							•		
Quail										•	•											•		
Redpoll	•			•																				
Robin							•	•	•	•			•	•					•	•	•			
Siskin, Pine	•				•																			•
Solitaire													•	•					•	•			•	
Sparrow, Fox					•	•													•	•		•		
Sparrow, Song					•								•		•									
Sparrow, Tree					•				•															
Sparrow, Wh.-throat.					•				•				•		•				•	•				
Starling			•					•					•	•	•									
Swallow, Tree			•											•	•									
Tanager			•				•	•	•				•	•	•				•					
Thrasher							•	•	•	•	•		•	•	•				•		•			
Thrush							•	•	•	•			•	•	•				•		•	•	•	
Titmice					•		•												•		•			
Towhee			•				•		•				•		•						•			
Vireo				•			•						•		•				•					
Warbler				•			•			•			•	•	•				•					
Waxwing, Cedar							•	•			•	•							•	•		•		
Woodpecker, Flicker				•	•		•	•		•			•	•	•				•	•	•	•	•	
Wren, Cactus															•									
Wren, Carolina				•																				

	Hickories	Hollies	Madrones, Pacific	Manzanita	Maples	Mesquite	Mountain Ash	Mulberries	Oaks	Palmetto	Pepper Tree, Calif.	Persimmon	Pines	Prickly Pear	Roses, Wild	Russian Olive	Serviceberry	Snowberry	Spruces	Sumacs	Sweet Gum	Tulip Tree	Virginia Creeper
Bluebird		•						•								•	•			•			•
Cardinal								•								•				•		•	
Catbird		•						•				•				•	•			•			
Chickadee							•					•					•		•		•		
Crossbill												•							•				
Duck, Wood	•							•															
Finch, Purple					•																•	•	
Flycatcher, Crested								•															•
Goldfinch					•																•	•	
Grosbeak	•				•		•	•	•			•			•	•	•		•	•			
Jay	•		•					•				•				•				•			
Junco												•				•				•			
Kingbird								•															
Mockingbird		•						•		•	•	•				•				•			
Nuthatch	•				•							•							•				•
Oriole								•									•						
Phainopepla											•												
Phoebe																			•				
Quail			•			•						•		•	•	•				•			
Redpoll																							
Robin							•	•		•	•	•				•	•			•			
Siskin, Pine													•						•				
Solitaire															•					•			
Sparrow, Fox			•																				•
Sparrow, Song																							
Sparrow, Tree																							
Sparrow, Wh.-throat.																					•		
Starling								•								•				•			
Swallow, Tree																							•
Tanager								•								•	•						
Thrasher		•						•	•					•	•	•				•			•
Thrush		•	•					•				•				•	•			•			•
Titmice							•					•											•
Towhee		•					•					•			•	•					•		
Vireo		•						•						•			•			•			•
Warbler								•			•	•	•							•			
Waxwing, Cedar		•					•				•	•			•	•			•				
Woodpecker; Flicker	•	•						•			•		•	•		•			•	•			
Wren, Cactus														•						•			
Wren, Carolina													•									•	

should be at least 6 feet wide, preferably more, if you wish birds to nest in them.

Plants for Your Region

The groups of plants in the table headings often have a number of different species and varieties. These will differ in different parts of the country. Your local nursery can usually tell you which will do best in your region. The United States Soil Conservation Service, your state forest service, or, in rural counties, the county agricultural agency may also be helpful. Write to your state agricultural college for its list of bulletins on what plants will grow best in your region.

The Planting Plan

John Terres, an authority on attracting birds, gives the following advice (see book list, page 118): If you want to make your yard or grounds more attractive to birds, first make a planting plan. You can make it yourself, or you can engage a landscape architect to make one for you. If you already have a garden, this plan should show you what plants to keep, which ones to dispose of, and what new plants to put in, and where.

You should decide first where to put the biggest plants; namely, trees and large shrubs. They usually go best in the background, near fence lines and in corners. Then plan where to put the smaller shrubs; then the vines and ground cover; and finally the flowers. In a flower bed put the tallest plants to the back and the smallest in front.

A good rule is to have at least 10 per cent of your plantings in evergreens. Put in plants both for bird food and for bird shelter. Place shelter plants near food-bearing plants so that feeding birds will have the safety of nearby shelter.

Plants that attract birds often have colorful flowers, fruits, berries, or autumn leaves. Thus they are attractive to man, too. Such plants will enhance the appearance of your grounds and the property value.

What Plants Different Birds Like for Food

The nationwide table (pp. 86-87) shows those plants that are of particular interest to well-known species of birds.

The heading "Bluebird" includes the eastern, western, and mountain bluebirds. "Mulberry" includes the red, white, and paper mulberry, and so on. Thus in any region the bluebird or bluebirds found there might be expected, in season, to feed on the fruit of the particular species of mulberry found there.

Flowers Whose Seeds Birds Like

The seeds of almost all flowers will be eaten by some seed-eating birds, but the seeds of these flowers are particular favorites:

Amaranthus	Chrysanthemum	Larkspur	Sorghum
Aster	Columbine	Marigold	Sunflower
Bachelor's Buttons	Coreopsis	Petunia	Sweet William
Bellflower	Cosmos	Phlox	Tarweed
Black-eyed Susan	Forget-me-not	Pink	Verbena
Calendula	Four-o'-clock	Poppy	Zinnia
Cardium	Gaillardia	Portulaca	

Bird Trees for Small Yards

If you have a small yard and want to put in a few trees that will attract birds, try one or more of the following:

Blue Beech	*Carpinus caroliniana*	Brazil Pepper Tree	*Schinus terebinthifolius*
Sugar Hackberry	*Celtis laevigata*	California Pepper Tree	*Schinus molle*
Pacific Madrone	*Arbutus menziesi*	Strawberry Tree	*Arbutus unedo*
	Amur Cork Tree[1]	*Phellodendron amurense*	

[1]For fruit you must have both a male and a female tree.

Some Fruits That Birds Like

(In general order of popularity)

Blackberry	*Rubus*	Huckleberry	*Gaylussacia*
Elderberry	*Sambucus*	Apple	*Malus*
Cherry, Wild	*Prunus*	Greenbrier	*Smilax*
Dogwood	*Cornus*	Crowberry	*Empetrum*
Sumac	*Rhus*	Rose	*Rosa*
Blueberry	*Vaccinium*	Serviceberry	*Amelanchier*
Grape	*Vitis*	Sour Gum	*Nyssa*
Mulberry	*Morus*	Hawthorn	*Crataegus*
Bayberry	*Myrica*	Virginia	*Parthenocissus*
Juniper	*Juniperus*	Creeper	
Pokeberry	*Phytolacca*	Snowberry	*Symphoricarpos*
Strawberry	*Fragaria*	Viburnum	*Viburnum*
Holly	*Ilex*	Bearberry	*Arctostaphylos*
Hackberry	*Celtis*		

Make a planting plan for your property. Lists in this chapter will tell you what plants are most attractive to birds. Since many of these plants have berries and leaves that are also attractive to man, they will improve the appearance of your grounds.

Flowers That Hummingbirds Like

Hummingbirds like bright trumpet- or tube-shaped flowers. Against a green background, red, orange, and purple are favorite colors. In desert regions birds will come to bright green flowers.

These are some of the kinds of flowers hummingbirds like:

Azalea	*Rhododendron*
Beardtongue	*Pentstemon*
Beebalm	*Monarda*
Bouncing Bet	*Saponaria*
Buckeye, Red (Horse Chestnut)	*Aesculus*
Butterfly Bush	*Buddleia*
Canna	*Canna*
Century Plant	*Agave*
Caestrum, Purple	*Caestrum*
Columbine	*Aquilegia*
Common Lantana	*Lantana*
Coral Bells	*Heuchera*
Day Lily	*Hemerocallis*
Eucalyptus	*Eucalyptus*
Fuschia	*Fuschia*
Geranium	*Pelargonium*
Gilia, Sweet	*Gilia*
Gladiolus	*Gladiolus*
Hawthorn	*Crataegus*
Hollyhock	*Althea*
Honeysuckle	*Lonicera*
Jasmine	*Jasminum*
Jewelweed	*Impatiens*
Larkspur	*Delphinium*
Lily	*Lilium*
Mallow (Scarlet Rose)	*Hibiscus*
Morning Glory	*Ipomoea*
Nasturtium	*Tropaeolum*
Orange Tree	*Citrus*
Ocotillo	*Fouquieria*
Paloverde	*Cercidium*
Petunia	*Petunia*
Pink	*Dianthus*
Ponciania, Royal	*Delonix*
Quince, Flowering Japanese	*Cydonia*
Rose	*Rosa*
Sage, Scarlet	*Salvia*
Scarlet Bush	*Hamelia*
Shrimp Plant	*Beloperone*
Siberian Pea Tree	*Caragana*
Silkoak	*Grevillea*
Silktree (Mimosa)	*Albizzia*
Spanish Bayonet	*Yucca*
Spiderflower	*Cleome*
Tree Tobacco	*Nicotiana*
Trumpet Creeper	*Bigonia*
Trumpet Vine	*Campsis*
Weigela	*Weigela*

TEN COMMON QUESTIONS AND ANSWERS
ABOUT BIRDS

1. How can I stop birds from hurting them-selves against my picture window?

Hang a few thin shimmering threads or aluminum ribbons from the eaves in front of the window. Or set up something that will cast a shadow on the window. Best of all, have a picture window that is tilted so that it will not reflect the landscape; then birds will not fly against it.

2. Should I let birds nest in my garage?

Certainly. But if you do, be sure you always leave the door or window open so they can get in and out.

3. A robin fights with its own image against our cellar window. How can we stop it?

Put a screen in front of the window.

4. What should I do if I find a nest blown out of a tree with the nestlings still alive?

Put the nest and birds in a small fruit bas-ket and hang the basket near the old location of the nest. The parents will almost certainly come back and feed them.

5. If I find a young bird that can't fly, what should I do?

If it has fallen out of its nest nearby, put it back. If you can't find the nest, leave the bird alone. Or, if a cat might get it, put it up on a bush. Its parents will almost certainly come back and feed it. They can't if you take it away.

6. If I find young birds that have no parents, how can I help them?

Consult members of your bird club who have successfully raised young birds. There is usually a "bird doctor" in every community, and his or her advice is valuable. As a general rule, feed young songbirds a mixture of mashed egg yolk and *moist* Pablum every 15 minutes for 12 hours a day. Do not give them water. You can add soft insects and worms to their diet, too. Keep them in a covered box for warmth.

7. I like birds and I like cats. How can I keep my cat from catching birds?

You can't, always. But you should bell the cat, feed it well, and not let it wander at large during the nesting season. Do not feed birds on the ground when the cat is around.

8. What should I do about blue jays?

Be glad you have some. Enjoy their beau-tiful colors, if they come to your feeder. Blue jays are noisy and quarrelsome, but they also act as sentinels, warning all wild creatures of danger.

9. Starlings roost on trees on my property. How can I get rid of them?

You probably can't; but you can try. Tie a rope around some of the branches of the trees, and shake them every evening when the birds are roosting. Or put up an imitation owl to frighten the starlings away. Consult other persons in your bird club who may have had some success with the same problem. Remem-ber, though, that starlings can be helpful to man—they eat Japanese beetles.

10. I have many house sparrows at my feeder. What can I do about them?

Very little. House sparrows tend to gather at feeders. It is legal to trap them and to re-lease them elsewhere. You can stop up their nesting holes, and otherwise try to discourage them from breeding near you. Or, you can try to enjoy them. Isn't it marvelous that a species is so bold that it has spread over North Amer-ica in just forty years?—and so adaptable that it thrives both in Death Valley and on Hudson Bay? Perhaps you can welcome a species that brings one of the few bird sounds that come to city-dwellers and shut-ins.

A bird's nest is replaced carefully.
Cy La Tour

PHOTOGRAPHING BIRDS

Bird photography is a popular part of bird watching, and there are few birders who have not tried it. If you like photography you will find that it is not difficult to take pictures of birds. However, birds are so active and shy that you must use special methods to bring them within range of the camera.

The joy of bird photography has been likened to the joy of hunting. But photography requires more skill and patience, because the camera has to be closer than the gun. Photography does not require the killing and the cruelty of crippling. It saves the birds for others to enjoy, and every season is open.

Many subjects for bird photography will occur to you as soon as you start taking pictures. One of the simplest shots is that of half-wild waterfowl on a pond, coming to be fed. If you have young children in your family, take a picture of them feeding the ducks or geese. Another favorite is of sparrows on the ground eating grain you have put out.

Attracting Birds

The easiest pictures to take are those of birds that come to you. The three standard ways to attract birds are with food, water, and bird houses.

Bird watchers who can imitate birds are often able to lure them toward the camera. "Squeaking" (kissing your hand) and the use of man-made bird calls are good ways of bringing birds close. But attracting by sounds does not always bring the birds right up to the camera as will food or water.

You can often get close to a bird at its nest. Either the incubating bird or the parents feeding the young makes a good photograph. But, for the sake of the birds, the photographing of nestlings should be left to the experts.

Tips and Shortcuts

Place your camera in front of a feeding station or bird bath; then the birds will come within range. Or the camera can be set up on a tripod near a bird house, if good light is available there. A natural-looking picture will result if you put food on the ground or stuff it into crevices on a tree, instead of using a feeder.

Bits of short, colored string placed in a hanging bird feeder or draped over a branch will attract orioles and other species looking for nesting material. Place such a "string depot" where you can take pictures of the birds using it. To attract wrens, try

Even if you live in the city you can get pictures of birds. This black and white photograph is an excellent example of what can be done with a city pigeon in the rain.

a little pile of slim twigs a few inches long, suitable for wren nests. A snapshot of a bird busy with construction materials is worth having.

If you fail in efforts to lure large birds, such as ducks, toward you, have a friend go around to the other side of the pond or marsh and make a disturbance to drive them in your direction.

Where the photographic conditions are difficult or doubtful, and when taking a picture of a rare bird or a bird in an unusual situation, take several shots. Try different light settings, to be sure that one will be right. Also shoot from various angles.

Keep a notebook if you want to improve your skill. After each shot, record such details as light, opening, speed, filter, film, and time of day. Later you can check the photographs against these data and see where your mistakes were.

Leave this type of picture—a portrait of a young least bittern—to the expert "birder"; otherwise you may endanger the life of the bird.

Helen Cruickshank—National Audubon Society

Some Possible Photographs

Close-ups

Birds at your feeding station
Hummingbirds at a hummingbird feeder
A sparrow in a dust bath
A bird at a bird box
An oriole collecting string for its nest
A pelican perched on a wharf or piling
Children feeding gulls, ducks, or swans at a beach or pond

At a little distance

A crow by the highway eating an animal killed by a car
Gulls following a boat (take the picture from the stern)
Seabirds following a "chum line" of food put out by birders

In flight

Ducks rising from the water
Gulls or hawks circling overhead
A tern, pelican, or gannet diving
Terns flying up and down the beach
Osprey carrying a fish
Gulls dropping clams to break the shell
Gulls at a sewer outlet
Pelicans or cormorants flying in formation low over the water
Crows coming into a roost

By stalking or with a blind

Shorebirds on a mud flat
Gulls at a garbage dump

camera for the distance you want, then wait till the bird flies into range. It is easier to obtain a good picture if the bird is coming head on, or at a slight angle, than if it is flying across in front of you.

Film and Camera

You may use either black-and-white or color film, and either still pictures or movies can be taken. Beginners usually start off with stills in black and white. These are the least expensive to practice with. It will take time for you to learn to use your camera under the special conditions of bird photography.

Various kinds of cameras are use-

ful, and each has its own virtues. Study the different kinds of cameras; ask the advice of your local camera dealer. Talk to other photographers in your bird club.

Unless you can get very close to your bird, the picture you get with a simple box camera will be too small.

A professional bird photographer "shoots" a baby tern on the beach.
Bartlett Hendricks—National Audubon Society

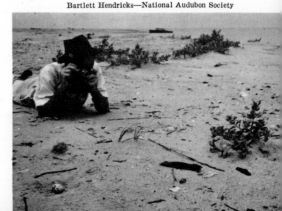

Helen Cruickshank—National Audubon Society

Noddy terns, found in the Dry Tortugas, off the coast of Florida, make a handsome picture. They are our only brown terns.

The same is true for 35 mm. and other small cameras unless you can use a telephoto lens. A wide-angle lens may be required when you need a wide field—for example, to cover shore birds on a long stretch of beach.

Your camera should have speeds of 1/300 second or faster to "stop" birds in flight. Even a bird on the ground or perching may be in con-

The 35 mm. camera with a fast shutter speed is probably best for most amateur bird photographers. You will also need a telescopic lens. Professionals often use a press camera, but this equipment is heavy to carry in the field.

A set-up for remote control photography (upper left) and two types of bird blinds.

stant jerky motion, demanding high speed for a clear picture. With high speed be sure to use sufficient aperture and accurate focusing.

In 35 mm., color pictures which can be projected will give more satisfaction than black-and-whites. For the finest work, professionals use a camera that will give 4 x 5 transparencies.

In bird photography a tripod is often a necessity. Have one handy whenever you can. A tripod is especially needed for slower pictures, which demand steadiness of the camera. For these, if you lack a tripod, you should steady the camera on something firm, such as a fence post, large branch, or stone wall. As a last resort, hold your breath, press the camera back firmly against your chest, and slowly squeeze the shutter release.

Sometimes you can borrow a camera and try it out for a while. When you are ready, buy as good and as sturdy a camera as you can afford. Field trips will give it lots of hard usage.

Good bird photography is not easy. Ingenuity, quick thinking, an understanding of bird behavior, and thorough knowledge of your camera —including light meter and filters— are vital. And for precisely these reasons bird photography can be a challenge and great fun.

Flash

Flash is standard equipment for night photography. It is useful by day, too, to bring out the color in a dull light or to balance the light. Since the camera must be set outside the blind, use flash that is synchronized with the shutter and that has remote control. Startle the bird into position with a faint click just before snapping the shutter.

Electronic flash of very short duration is now used by experienced bird photographers. Exposures as short as 1/10,000 of a second can be obtained. But even 1/5,000 is enough. With such speeds you can stop the motion of a bird's wing. However, electronic flash is still expensive and complicated.

Motion Pictures

Increasing numbers of people are taking color movies of birds. Movies show the characteristic traits and behavior patterns of a bird that appear only in its motions. Many fascinating examples of bird behavior can be captured by motion pictures.

Movie cameras have lenses ranging from wide angle to 1000 mm. A tripod and a telephoto lens are essential. Movie cameras are, of course, more expensive and heavier than still cameras of a comparable size.

A special advantage of motion pictures is that, if carefully planned, they can be made up into a continuous documentary film eventually.

For more information on the fascinating subject of how to become a bird photographer, consult Allan D. Cruickshank's practical *Hunting with a Camera.*

A family of young crows makes an appealing picture.

Helen Cruickshank—National Audubon Society

G. Ronald Austing—National Audubon Society

An apprehensive saw-whet owl is banded.

BIRD BANDING

Bird banding, or the placing of metal bands on birds' legs, is done so that scientists can learn about migrations, life spans, and wanderings. The persons who put these bands on are called bird banders.

Banders and Their Work

Each bander must have a federal permit and a state permit. To obtain this permit an applicant has to be at least 18 years old and must furnish references from at least three well-known ornithologists, naturalists, or banders. Each applicant is carefully investigated, not only for general fitness but in particular for his ability to identify birds. There are about 2,000 banders in the United States and about 500 in Canada.

Bird banders, like bird watchers, come from all walks of life. They include professional ornithologists, housewives, and businessmen. They have the satisfaction of adding to scientific knowledge.

The Fish and Wildlife Service of the United States Department of the Interior and the Canadian Wildlife

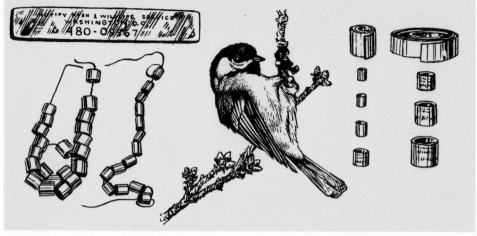

There are bird bands to fit on the leg of almost any size of bird.

Service administer the bird-banding program. They grant the permits and supply banders with free, numbered aluminum bands in different sizes. They also supply the forms that have to be filled out and filed with the government to show what birds have been banded.

If you find a dead bird with a band on its leg, send the band to: Bird Banding Office, Patuxent Research Refuge, U.S. Fish and Wildlife Service, Laurel, Maryland. Tell them where and when you found the bird. If you include your name and address, this office will notify you where the bird was banded and when. It will also notify the bander of the date and place where the band was recovered.

Bird banding provides the U.S. Fish and Wildlife Service with information about the age and habits of waterfowl and other birds. This helps them in determining hunting regulations each year.

Banding Then and Now

Audubon was the first known American bird bander. In 1803 he put silver threads around the legs of some nestling phoebes near his farm at Mill Grove, Pennsylvania. The next year, two of these "banded" birds came back and nested in a nearby cave.

Modern banding began in the United States in 1902, when Dr. Paul Bartsch of the Smithsonian Institution banded 23 black-crowned night herons. The first "long-distance" recovery was in 1905, when one of Bartsch's herons, banded in 1903, was found dead in Cuba. In 1920 bird banding was brought under the auspices of the government.

To date more than 11,000,000 birds of North America have been banded — 750,000 in 1959 alone. About 50,000 bands are recovered each year.

Some Banding Records

There are some interesting records on banded birds. One arctic tern, banded as a chick beside the Elbe River in Germany in 1920, was killed by a cat 26 years later when nesting on an island near its birthplace.

Another arctic tern chick, banded at Turnavik Bay, Labrador, on July 23, 1928, was found dead four months later at Port Shepstone, Natal, Union of South Africa, a distance of 10,000 miles as the tern flies. A homing record of 3,200 miles was made by a Manx shearwater taken from its Skokholm, Wales, burrow and released at Boston, Massachusetts. It was back in its burrow again in 12½ days!

Banding has shown that some birds fly east and west rather than north and south. A pintail duck banded in 1953 in Alberta was shot in 1957 at Matsushima Bay, Japan. More than a hundred birds, mostly pintails and lesser snow geese, banded in North America have been recovered in Siberia by the Soviet bird-banding organization.

Waterfowl and other game birds account for about 25 per cent of all birds banded. More than 958,000 mallards alone have been ringed. Bands from 170,000 have been reported—a return of 17 per cent. This is more than double the average return for all banded birds.

Banders of chimney swifts hold the

John H. Gerard—National Audubon Society
A young black-crowned night heron is banded at a banding station.

record for numbers of individual birds banded in one day at one station —5,400. In this case, the swifts were in migration and roosting by the thousands in one chimney. Banders closed the chimney top after dark with tarpaulin. At dawn they lifted one corner of the tarpaulin and connected it with a funnel and a stovepipe that led to a gathering cage. As the swifts flew out in the morning, they were diverted into the cages for banding.

For a long time the winter home of the chimney swift was unknown. In December 1943, however, metal bands were taken from the legs of some "swallows" killed by Indians near the Yanayaco River in eastern

All duck banding is done by representatives of the U.S. Fish and Wildlife Service.

Rex Gary Schmidt—U.S. Fish and Wildlife Service

Peru. The United States Embassy in Lima forwarded these bands to Washington. Twelve bands had been placed on chimney swifts in Tennessee; one swift was banded in Ontario. Through recovery of bands, scientists had finally learned where chimney swifts spent the winter.

Banding Methods

In the early days of bird banding, many young birds were banded in the nest, because this was so easy. Unfortunately, few birds survived, partly because the activity of banding attracted predators to the nest. For this and other reasons banding of nestling songbirds is frowned on.

Banding of colonial nesting birds, however, such as gulls and terns, has been quite successful. But it is best carried out by professionals or advanced banders. The banding of waterfowl is almost entirely a government operation.

The private individual bander is today responsible for the bulk of nongame bird banding. He usually maintains traps in the yard of his home. Often the traps can be seen from the kitchen window. Traps may be of various kinds and are usually baited with grain or water and put in operation only at times when someone is on hand to service them. Birds should

duck trap

pheasant trap

Types of nets and traps used by experts to capture birds for banding.

sparrow trap

waterfowl nets

mist net

banding equipment

not be kept in a trap for more than 15 or 30 minutes.

When the banding is done, the date, name of the species, and the number of the band is written on the band.

The latest thing in banding is the mist net. This is a fine, nearly invisible net about 35 feet long and 3 to 7 feet high. Attached to upright poles, the net is set across paths, woods, roads, and open spaces in the migration flyways of land birds. The net catches many species of insect-eating birds that will not come to grain-baited traps.

To operate a mist net, the bird bander must have a special authorization added to his regular banding permit. Nets require greater skill to operate than ground traps. They are opening up fascinating new vistas on migration. But mist nets must be operated by advanced bird banders.

Making Reports

Reports on banded birds are of four kinds. A *recovery* is a banded bird that is shot or found dead. A *foreign retrap* is a bird trapped that had already been banded at a different location. A *return* is a bird that returns to the original bander's trap after a period of 90 days. A *repeat* is a bird that returns to the original bander in less than 90 days. Some birds seem to get "trap-

happy" and come back again and again to the same trap.

Information on each recovery, retrap, and return (but not repeat) must be filed with the Bird Banding Office of the Fish and Wildlife Service at Laurel, Maryland.

Organizations and Their Memberships

Bird banders in the United States are organized into four regional Bird Banding Associations (BBA) as follows:

Northeastern BBA: c/o Mrs. James R. Downs, S. Londonderry, Vermont

Eastern BBA: c/o Mrs. John C. Schmid, 24 Bowman Dr., Greenwich, Conn.

Inland BBA: c/o P. R. Macklin, 666 West High St., Berne, Indiana

Western BBA: c/o T. E. Balch, Glenn (Glenn Co.), California

The official journal of North American bird banding is *Bird Banding* (c/o Alexander Bergstrom, 370 Old Brook Road, W. Hartford 7, Conn.), published by the Northeastern BBA.

Only the very best qualified applicants can become banders. If you want to become one, talk to a bird bander in your local bird club, or write your regional bird-banding association for the names of banders in your area. Talk to them. If they feel you are qualified, they will tell you how to apply for a permit and how to begin work.

Common egrets were saved from extinction through the efforts of the Audubon Society.

CONSERVATION

Anyone interested in birds hopes that there will always be plenty of birds to enjoy, and for his children to enjoy after him. But there will be only if we practice wise conservation.

Birds of Yesteryear

In the last century the hunter was the big threat to birds. Market hunting, plume hunting, too much hunting; collecting of nests and eggs; insufficient and poorly enforced game laws—all these destroyed billions of birds. Several species were wiped out altogether.

The great auk, a large flightless water bird, used for food and for feathers, was totally destroyed by 1844. The last passenger pigeon died in the Cincinnati Zoo in 1914. Their vast flights had once darkened the sun. Alexander Wilson, an early American ornithologist, estimated that there were 2,230,272,000 pigeons in one flock which he saw in Kentucky in 1810.

The beautiful Carolina parakeet

To encourage young people to take an interest in nature is to enrich their lives.

was shot to extinction by 1920. The last heath hen died in 1931. Thousands of Eskimo curlews once blanketed the prairies in migration, and were mercilessly slaughtered. One solitary individual, perhaps the last of its species, was reported from Texas in April, 1959.

The Conservation Movement

Long, hard fights by the Audubon Society and other conservation organizations over the last sixty years have done much to save our birds. Strict game laws have spared our waterfowl. Complete protection has saved the shore birds from extinction. Laws finally put a stop to plume hunt-

ing for ladies' hats, but not until two Audubon wardens had been murdered by plume hunters.

An international treaty with Canada safeguards our migratory birds. Hawks and owls, great mouse-destroyers for the farmer, are gradually receiving better protection. Collecting of birds' nests and eggs is now forbidden.

Our Homeless Birds

The man with the gun is not the main danger today. Today's main danger is the man with the bulldozer. Construction of ever more roads, buildings, and factories means fewer bird homes in fields and woods and swamps. It is this loss of homes, or habitat, that most seriously threatens birds today. If we destroy a bird's home we destroy the bird, as surely as if we shot it.

The California condor, large bird of prey, is now confined to one wilderness area in southern California. The ivory-billed woodpecker may—or may not—still linger on in a few virgin swamps in the South. Excessive drainage and settlement have greatly reduced the numbers of the Everglade kite in Florida.

With the growth of cities and industry, destruction of habitat is going on at an increasing rate. Furthermore, wetlands, with all their peculiar species of swamp, marsh, and meadow, are threatened by constant drainage and filling. Shores and beaches also are menaced by the growth of summer resorts. Habitat, therefore, is the most important thing to save, if we are to save our birds.

Commercial spraying with deadly insecticides is another threat. These poisons are becoming stronger each year. We are uncertain whether the birds die from eating poisoned insects, starve from lack of insects to eat, or are driven away. But we know that the songbird population is drastically reduced after an area is heavily sprayed with chemical pesticides.

What We Can Do

What can we do to save our birds?

The first thing is to join an organization that is working for wildlife and nature protection.

Certain of these organizations are listed on page 111. Some of them work on a national level to guard against encroachment on lands already set aside as parks or wild areas. They also help in getting laws passed to provide for more areas of this type in order to take care of our ever-increasing population.

The second most useful step is to see what needs to be done locally. Join your local bird club or other or-

Maurice Broun

Owls and hawks are important in the balance of nature. In many states they are now protected by law as are songbirds.

ganization that is interested in conservation. Take an active part in its program. Find out the local conservation issues that need attention.

Does your state need a model hawk-and-owl law? Does your county need more park land or wetlands? Is spraying with powerful insecticides destroying birds and other wildlife in your area?

Has your community set aside a sufficiently large area as a wildlife sanctuary? Do your schools need more land for nature study? Has your town preserved at least one fresh-water marsh or a big enough stretch of salt marsh? Are billboards ruining the beauty of your highways? Does your town need a young people's nature center?

Some of these may already be important issues in your community. If so, it is possible you can help in that particular campaign. In many cases study is required to see what is needed along these lines in a given area.

You might join or start a conservation committee in your local bird club. Such a committee should decide which are the most essential local conservation issues. It should do research on them in order to inform other club members and your local newspaper about them. It could start a campaign to correct them.

Most bird watchers enjoy working for the protection of birds and nature. If, for example, you help set up a local wildlife sanctuary and nature center, you will have made a permanent contribution to the community. It will be a lifelong source of satisfaction to you. And your children and grandchildren may well bless you for it.

Our first National Park was Yellowstone, established in 1872. We now have twenty-nine National Parks which include more than thirteen million acres of land. These parks are a priceless heritage which belong to all the people. The parks are wildlife sanctuaries and no shooting is allowed in them. This is a scene in Glacier National Park in Montana.

LEADING WILDLIFE CONSERVATION AGENCIES

Name	Works to Protect
National Audubon Society 1130 Fifth Ave., New York 28, N. Y.	Soil, water, plants, birds and wildlife
National Wildlife Federation 1412 16th St. N.W., Washington, D. C.	Wildlife
Emergency Conservation Committee 767 Lexington Ave., New York, N. Y.	Immediately threatened species
Hawk Mountain Sanctuary Association, Kempton, Pa.	Hawks and wildlife
Nature Conservancy 2015 Bunker Hill Rd. N.E., Washington 18, D. C.	Significant natural areas threatened by development
National Parks Association 1300 New Hampshire Ave. N.W., Washington 7, D. C.	National parks and monuments
Wilderness Society, 2144 P St. N.W., Washington, D. C.	Wilderness
Sierra Club 1050 Mills Tower, San Francisco 4, Calif.	Mountains, national parks, wilderness

Edward Prins

The cardinal, our only crested, all-red bird, is the state bird of seven states—Illinois, Indiana, Kentucky, North Carolina, Ohio, Virginia, and West Virginia.

ciety has an annual convention each November with a similar program. State and local societies usually have an annual meeting or dinner. Joining such societies and attending their conventions is an excellent way of keeping up with what is going on in the "bird world," and of meeting fellow bird watchers and professional ornithologists.

LOCAL BIRD CLUBS

UNITED STATES

Alabama — *Birmingham:* Birmingham Aud. Soc. *Montgomery:* Montgomery Aud. Soc. **Arizona**—*Phoenix:* Maricopa Aud. Soc. *Tucson:* Tucson Aud. Soc. **Arkansas**—*Fort Smith:* Fort Smith Aud. Soc. *Little Rock:* Pulaski County Aud. Soc. **California**—*Burlingame:* Sequoia Aud. Soc. *Carlsbad:* Buena Vista Aud. Soc. *Carmel:* Monterey Peninsula Aud. Soc. *Claremont:* Pomona Valley Aud. Soc. *Fullerton:* Sea and Sage Aud. Soc. *Larkspur:* Marin Aud. Soc. *Los Altos:* Santa Clara Valley Aud. Soc. *Los Angeles:* Los Angeles Aud. Soc. *Pasadena:* Pasadena Aud. Soc. *Paso Robles:* Paso Robles Aud. Soc. *Ross:* Marin Conservation League

Sacramento: Sacramento Aud. Soc. *San Bernardino:* San Bernardino Valley Aud. Soc. *San Diego:* San Diego Aud. Soc. *San Francisco:* Golden Gate Aud Soc. *Stockton:* Stockton Aud. Soc. *Sun Valley:* San Fernando Valley Aud. Soc. *Turlock:* Stanislaus County Wildlife Soc. *Walnut Creek:* Mount Diablo Aud. Soc. *Whittier:* Whittier Aud. Soc. **Colorado**—*Boulder:* Boulder Bird Club. *Colorado Springs:* Aiken Ornithological Soc. **Connecticut**—*Bristol:* Terryville Nat. History Club. *Fairfield:* Aud. Soc. of Conn. *Greenwich:* Greenwich Aud. Soc. *Morris:* Litchfield Hills Aud. Soc. *Sharon:* Housatonic Aud. Soc. *Stamford:* Stamford Museum and Nature Center. *Storrs:* Natchaug Ornithological Soc. *Waterbury:* Waterbury Naturalists Club, Inc. *Westport:* Westport Aud. Soc. **District of Columbia**—*Washington:* Audubon Naturalist Society of D. C., Inc. **Florida**—*Bradenton:* Manatee County Aud. Soc. *Clearwater:* Clearwater Aud. Soc. *Clewiston:* Lake Okeechobee Aud. Soc. *Daytona Beach:* Halifax River Aud. Club *De Land:* Seminole Aud. Soc. *Fort Lauderdale:* Broward County Aud. Soc. *Fort Myers:* Southwest Florida Aud. Soc. *Fort Pierce:* Saint Lucie Aud. Soc. *Jacksonville:* Duval County Aud. Soc. *Miami:* Tropical Aud. Soc. *Rockledge:* Indian River Aud. Soc. *St. Petersburg:* St. Petersburg Aud. Soc. *Sanibel:* Sanibel Captiva Aud. Soc. *Tavernier:* Monroe County Aud. Soc. *West Palm Beach:* Audubon Soc. of the Everglades. **Georgia**—*Athens:* Athens Bird Club *Atlanta:* Atlanta Bird Club. *Augusta:* Augusta

Bird Club. *Milledgeville:* Milledgeville Aud. Soc. *Rome:* Floyd County Aud Soc.; Georgia Ornithological Soc. *Savannah:* Savannah Aud. Soc. **Hawaii**—*Honolulu:* Hawaii Aud. Soc.; Hui Manu Club. **Illinois**—*Champaign:* Champaign County Aud. Club, Inc. *Danville:* Vermillion County Aud. Soc. *Decatur:* Decatur Aud. Soc. *Elgin:* Elgin Aud. Soc. *Evanston:* Evanston Bird Club. *Glen Ellyn:* Benjamin T. Gault Bird Club. *Highland Park:* Illinois Aud. Soc. *Olney:* Ridgway Bird Club of Olney. *Princeton:* Bureau Valley Aud. Club. *Sterling:* White Pines Bird Club. *Wheaton:* Du Page Aud. Soc. **Indiana** —*Evansville:* Lida Edwards Aud. Soc. *Hanover:* Indiana Aud. Soc. *Lafayette:* Purdue Univ. Bird Study Group. *Mishawaka:* Aud. Naturalists of Saint Joseph Valley; South Bend Aud. Soc. *Mooresville:* Amos W. Butler Chapter, Indiana Aud. Soc. *Richmond:* Richmond Aud. and Nature Club **Iowa**—*Cedar Falls:* Cedar Falls Aud. Soc. *Des Moines:* Des Moines Aud. Soc. *Farley:* Dubuque Aud. Club. *Newton:* Iowa Ornithologists Union. *Rock Island:* Tri-City Bird Club. *Sioux City:* Sioux City Bird Club. *Waterloo:* Waterloo Aud. Soc. **Kansas**— *Edgerton:* Baldwin Bird Club. *Mound City:* Linn County Aud. Soc. *Pleasanton:* Kansas Ornithological Society. *Topeka:* Topeka Aud. Soc. *Wichita:* Wichita Aud. Soc. **Kentucky**— *Henderson:* Henderson Aud. Soc. *Lexington:* Aud. Soc. of Kentucky. *Louisville:* Beckham Bird Club. *Madisonville:* Kentucky Ornithological Soc. **Louisiana**—*New Orleans:* Orleans Aud. Soc. *Shreveport:* Louisiana Ornithological Soc. **Maine**—*Bangor:* Bangor Bird Conservation Club. *Bar Harbor:* Mount Desert Island Bird Club. *Lewiston:* Stanton Bird Club. *Wayne:* The Maine Aud. Soc. **Maryland**—*Baltimore:* Maryland Ornithological Soc. *Chestertown:* Kent County Chapter, Maryland Ornithological Soc. *Cumberland:* Allegany Bird Club. *Easton:* Talbot County Bird Club. *Frederick:* Frederick Branch, Maryland Ornithological Society *Greensboro:* Caroline County Bird Club. *Havre de Grace:* Hartford County Bird Club. *Owings Mills:* Baltimore Bird Club, Maryland Ornithological Soc. **Massachusetts**—*Amherst:* Eliot Bird Club. *Boxford:* Essex County Ornithological Club. *Lincoln:* Massachusetts Aud. Soc. *Monson:* Allen Bird Club. *Pittsfield:* Hoffman Bird Club. *Rockport:* Brookline Bird Club **Michigan** — *Allendale:* Grand Rapids Aud. Club. *Ann Arbor:* Washtenaw Aud. Soc. *Midland:* Michigan Aud. Soc. *Mount Pleasant:* Chippewa Valley Aud. Club. *Royal Oak:* Detroit

Aud. Soc. **Minnesota**—*Albert Lea:* Albert Lea Aud. Soc. *Duluth:* Duluth Bird Club. *Mankato:* Mankato Aud. Soc.; Minnesota Ornithologists Union. *Minneapolis:* Minneapolis Aud. Soc.; Minnesota Bird Club. *St. Paul:* Minneapolis Bird Club; St. Paul Aud. Soc. **Mississippi**— *Laurel:* Laurel Aud. Soc. **Missouri**—*Jefferson City:* Aud. Soc. of Missouri *St. Joseph:* St. Joseph Aud. Soc. *St. Louis:* St. Louis Aud. Soc. **Montana**—*Billings:* Billings Aud. Soc. *Great Falls:* Rainbow Bird Club *Livingston:* Sacajawea Aud. Soc. **Nebraska**—*Beatrice:* Beatrice Aud. Soc. *Lincoln:* University Place Bird Club *Wisner:* Nebraska Ornithologists Union. **New Hampshire**—*Dublin:* Aud. Soc. of New Hampshire. **New Jersey**—*Fairlawn:* Hackensack Aud. Soc. *Flemington:* Hunterdon County Bird Club *Franklin Lake:* New Jersey Aud. Soc. *Haddonfield:* Aud. Wildlife Soc. *Montclair:* Montclair Bird Club. *Newark:* Urner Ornithological Club *New Lisbon:* Pemberton Bird Club. *Ridgewood:* Ridgewood Aud. Soc. *Westfield:* Watchung Nature Club; Westfield Bird Club. **New York**—*Amityville:* Baldwin Bird Club. *Amsterdam:* Sassafras Bird Club. *Bedford:* Bedford Aud. Soc. *Catskill:* Greene County Bird Club. *East Aurora:* Buffalo Ornithological Soc. *East Chatham:* Alan Devoe Bird Club. *Elmira:* Chemung Valley Aud. Soc. *Hastings-on-Hudson:* Hastings Humane Soc., Inc. *Haverstraw:* Rockland County Conservation Assoc. *Jamestown:* Jamestown Aud. Soc. *Kenmore:* Buffalo Aud. Soc. *Keuka Park:* Keuka Park Conservation Club *Monticello:* Sullivan County Aud. Soc. *New York City:* (Brooklyn) Brooklyn Bird Club (Queens) Queens County Bird Club. (Manhattan) Linnaean Soc. (Staten Island) Staten Island Institute of Arts & Science, Natural History Section. *Nyack:* Rockland Aud. Soc. *Plandome:* Lyman Langdon Aud. Soc. *Pleasantville:* Saw Mill River Aud. Soc. *Rensselaerville:* Edmund Niles Huyck Preserve, Inc. *Rochester:* Burroughs Aud. Nature Club; Federation of New York State Bird Clubs; Genesee Ornithological Soc. of New York. *Scarsdale:* Scarsdale Aud. Soc. *Schenectady:* Schenectady Bird Club, Inc. *Sparrow Bush:* Minisink Aud. Soc. *Syracuse:* Onondaga Aud. Soc. *Wappingers Falls:* Ralph T. Waterman Bird Club. *Watertown:* North Country Bird Club. *Watkins Glen:* Watkins Montour Bird Club. **North Carolina**— *Charlotte:* Cardinal Bird Club; Mecklenburg Aud. Club. *Greensboro:* Piedmont Bird Club Chapel Hill Bird Club. *Lenoir:* Lenoir Aud. *Henderson:* Henderson Bird Club. *Hillsboro:*

Club *Raleigh:* Raleigh Bird Club. *Tryon:* Tryon Bird Club. *Wilmington:* Carolina Bird Club **North Dakota**—*Bismarck:* Bismarck Aud. Soc. *Kenmare:* Kenmare Bird Club. **Ohio**—*Akron:* Cuyahoga Falls ·Aud. Club. *Cincinnati:* Aud. Soc. of Ohio. *Cleveland:* Cleveland Aud. Soc. *Columbus:* Columbus Aud. Soc. *Dayton:* Dayton Aud. Soc. *Elyria:* Elyria Aud. Soc. *Mansfield:* Kellogg Aud. Club. *Painesville:* Blackbrook Aud. Soc. *Steubenville:* Forest Aud. Club *Toledo:* Toledo Naturalists' Assoc. *Zanesville:* Zanesville Aud. Soc. **Oklahoma** — *Norman:* Cleveland County Bird Club; Okla. Ornithological Society. *Oklahoma City:* Okla. City Aud. Soc. *Tulsa:* Tulsa Aud. Soc. **Oregon**—*Forest Grove:* Forest Grove Bird Study Group. *Portland:* Oregon Aud. Soc. **Pennsylvania**—*Allentown:* Lehigh Valley Bird Club. *Bethlehem:* Moravian College Conservation Assoc. *Harvey's Lake:* The Back Mountain Bird Club. *Lancaster:* Lancaster County Bird Club. *Norristown:* Aud. Club of Norristown. *Philadelphia:* Bird Club of Philadelphia; Delaware Valley Ornithological Club; Pennypack Valley Bird Club; The Comstock Soc. *Pittsburgh:* Aud. Soc. of Western Pennsylvania. *Sayre:* Susquehanna Valley Aud. Soc. *Scranton:* Scranton Bird Club *Sewickley:* Aud. Soc. of Sewickley Valley. *State College:* State College Bird Club. *Wellsboro:* Tiadaghton Aud. Soc. *West Chester:* West Chester Bird Club. *Wyncote:* Wyncote Bird Club *Wyomissing:* Baird Ornithological Club. *York:* York County Bird Club. **Rhode Island**—*Barrington:* Aud. Soc. of Rhode Island. *Kingston:* Little Rest Bird Club.*Providence:* Prouts Neck Aud. Soc. **South Carolina**—*Columbia:* Columbia Bird Club.*Darlington:* Darlington Bird Club *Greenville:* Greenville Bird Club. **South Dakota**—*Huron:* Huron Bird Club. *Rapid City:* Black Hills Aud. Soc. *Sioux Falls:* Sioux Falls Aud. Soc.; South Dakota Ornithological Union **Tennessee** — *Chattanooga:* Chattanooga Aud. Soc. **Texas**—*Amarillo:* Texas Panhandle Aud. Soc. *Austin:* Travis Aud. Soc. *Dallas:* Dallas Aud. Soc. *El Paso:* El Paso Aud. Soc. *Fort Worth:* Fort Worth Aud. Soc. *McAllen:* Lower Rio Grande Valley Aud. Soc. *Palestine:* Texas Ornithological Soc. *San Antonio:* San Antonio Aud. Soc. *Tyler:* Tyler Aud. Soc. *Wichita Falls:* Wichita Falls Aud. Soc. **Utah**—*Salt Lake City:* Utah Aud. Soc. **Vermont**—*Bennington:* Vermont Bird Club.**Virginia**—*Hampton:* Hampton Roads Bird Club. *Norfolk:* Cape Henry Bird Club; Va. Soc. of Ornithology. **Washington**—*Des Moines:* Wesley Garden Aud. Club. *Olym-*

pia: Olympia Aud. Soc. *Pullman:* Pacific Northwestern Bird and Mammal Soc. *Seattle:* Seattle Aud. Soc. *Spokane:* Spokane Bird Club. **West Virginia**—*Huntington:* Huntington Bird Club *Wheeling:* Brooks Bird Club. **Wisconsin**—*Appleton:* Appleton Aud. Soc. *Beloit:* Ned Hollister Bird Club.*Grantsburg:* Burnett County Aud. Soc. *Madison:* Madison Aud. Soc. *Milwaukee:* Milwaukee Aud. Soc.; Wisconsin Soc. for Ornithology. **Wyoming** — *Casper:* Wyoming Aud. Soc.

CANADA

(This is only a partial list and includes natural history clubs. There are many more local clubs in Canada.)

Alberta—*Calgary:* Calgary Bird Club. *Edmonton:* Edmonton Bird Club. **British Columbia** —*Vancouver:* Vancouver Natural History Soc. *Victoria:* Victoria Natural Hist. Soc. **Manitoba** —*Winnipeg:* Manitoba Natural History Soc. **Newfoundland**—*St. John's:* Natural History Soc. of Newfoundland. **Nova Scotia**—*Halifax:* Nova Scotia Bird Soc. **Ontario**—*Ottawa:* Ottawa Field Naturalists' Club. *Toronto:* Aud. Soc. of Canada; Brodie Club; Federation of Ontario Naturalists; Toronto Field Naturalists' Club; Toronto Ornithological Club. **Quebec**—*Montreal:* Province of Quebec Soc. for the Protection of Birds. *Quebec City:* Club des Ornithologues; Provancher Soc. **Saskatchewan**—*Regina:* Saskatchewan Natural History Soc.

ORNITHOLOGICAL SOCIETIES ABROAD

Listed below are the best centers in various countries for bird-watching activities. In other countries contact the principal natural history museum.

Argentina—Sociedad Ornitologica del Plata, Ave. Angel Callardo 470, Buenos Aires. **Australia** — Royal Australasian Ornithologists' Union, 386 Flinders Lane, Melbourne. **Austria**—Verein Oesterreichische Vogelwarte, Verbund für Vogelkunde und Vogelschutz, Vienna 1, Burgring 7. **Bulgaria**—Centrale Ornithologique, Jardin Zoologique, Sofia. **Ceylon**—Ceylon Bird Club, c/o Colombo Museum, Colombo. **Czechoslovakia**—Ceskoslovenská Ornithologická Spolecmost, Praha 2, Václavské nám. **Denmark**—Dansk Ornithologisk Forening c/o Zoologiske Museum, Krystalgade, Copenhagen. **Eire**—Irish Ornithologists' Club, 5-6 Dame St., Dublin. **Finland**—Ornitologiska Föreningen i Finland, Helsinki, P. Rautatiek 13. **France**—(1) Société Orni-

Peter Post

Some birds, such as the kittiwake, can be seen both in North America and in northern Europe.

thologique de France et de l'Union Française, 55 rue de Buffon, Paris V. (2) Ligue pour la Protection des Oiseaux, 129 Boulevard St. Germain, Paris VI. **Holland**—Nederlandse Ornithologische Vereniging, c/o Zoologische Museum, Plantage Middenlaan 53, Amsterdam (C). **Hungary**—Association of Hungarian Ornithologists, c/o Ornithological Section, Research Institute of Plant Protection Garas–U 14, Budapest 11. **India**—Delhi Bird Watching Society, Kashmir House, New Delhi. **Israel**—Ornithological Society of Israel, Biological Institute, Jehuda Halevi 12, Tel-Aviv. **Italy**—Associazione Ornitologica Italiana, Via Belfiore 11, Milan. **Japan**—Ornithological Society of Japan c/o Yamashina Museum of Birds, 49 Nanpeidai-Machi, Shibuya-ku, Tokyo. **Luxembourg**—Ligue Luxembourgeoise pour l'Etude et la Protection des Oiseaux, 2 Rue Clémenceau, Luxembourg. **Morocco**—Association Ornithologique du Maroc, Institut Scientifique Chérifien, Avenue Biernay, Rabat. **New Zealand**—Ornithological Society of New Zealand, 22 Benbow St., St. Heliers, Auckland. **Spain**—Sociedad Española de Ornitologia, Castellana 84, Madrid. **Norway**—Norsk Ornitologisk Forening, Stavanger Museum, Stavanger. **Sweden** — Sveriges Ornitologiska Förening, Box 18081, Stockholm 19. **Switzerland** — ALA Schweizerische Gesllschaft für Vogelkunde und Vogelschutz, Bern. **Union of South Africa**—South African Ornithological Society, Box 1616, Cape Town. **Union of Soviet Sociaist Republics** — Ornithological Section, Russian Society for the Protection of Nature, Moscow, Wladimirskogo 6. **United Kingdom** —(1) British Ornithologists' Union, c/o Bird Room, British Museum (Natural History), Cromwell Rd., London S.W. 7. (2) British Trust for Ornithology, 2 King Edward St., Oxford. (3) Edward Grey Institute of Field Ornithology, Botanic Garden, High St., Oxford. (4) Royal Society for the Protection of Birds, 25 Eccleston Sq., London S.W. 1. (5) Scottish Society for the Protection of Birds, 135 Wellington St., Glasgow, C.2 (6) Ulster Society for the Protection of Birds, 6 Fitzwilliam St., Belfast, N. Ireland. (7) Wildfowl Trust, Slimbridge, Glos. **Yugoslavia**—Ornitoloski Zavod, Zagreb, Ilirski trg 9.

Two avocets here are walking on a mud flat in California. They are found chiefly in the West.

USEFUL REFERENCES

Attracting Birds
Songbirds in Your Garden, J. K. Terres (Crowell, New York, 1953), 274 pp.

Binoculars
Know Your Binoculars, R. J. & E. Reichert (Mirakel Optical, Mount Vernon, N.Y., 1951), 12 pp.

Bird Banding
Manual for Bird Banding, F. C. Lincoln (Fish & Wildlife Service, Washington, 1947), 116 pp.

Bird Finding
A Guide to Bird Finding East of the Mississippi, O. S. Pettingill, Jr. (Oxford Univ. Press, New York, 1951), 659 pp.
A Guide to Bird Finding West of the Mississippi, same, 1953, 709 pp.

Bird Watching
How to Watch Birds, R. Barton (McGraw-Hill, New York, 1955), 229 pp.
A Guide to Bird Watching, J. J. Hickey (Oxford Univ. Press, New York, 1943; Garden City reprint, 1953), 264 pp.

Conservation
Wildlife Conservation, I. N. Gabrielson (Macmillan, New York, 1959), 244 pp.

Drawing Birds
How to Draw Birds, L. B. Hunt
Techniques of Drawing and Painting Wildlife, (Reinhold, New York, 1960) 144 pp.

Evolution and Taxonomy
The A.O.U. Check-list of North American Birds, 5th ed. (American Ornithologists' Union, Fernow Hall, Cornell Univ., Ithaca, N.Y., 1957), 691 pp.

Field Guides
Complete Field Guide to American Wildlife; East, Central, North, H. H. Collins, Jr. (Harpers, New York, 1959), 683 pp. Includes birds, all other vertebrates, and chief marine invertebrates north of North Carolina and Oklahoma, and east of the Rockies.
The Pocket Guide to Birds, A. D. Cruickshank (Dodd, Mead, New York, 1953), 216 pp.; west to the Plains.

Birds, Gabrielson & Zim (Golden Press, New York, 1956), 155 pp., full-color plates of 125 species; identifies 250 American birds.
A Field Guide to the Birds, R. T. Peterson (Houghton Mifflin, Boston, 1947), 290 pp.; west to the Plains.
A Field Guide to Western Birds, same, 1941, 240 pp.; Plains to the Pacific.
Audubon Bird Guide, R. H. Pough (Doubleday, New York, 1946), 312 pp.; land birds west to the Plains.
Audubon Water Bird Guide, same, 1951, 352 pp.; west to the Plains.
Audubon Western Bird Guide, same, 1957, 316 pp.; Plains to the Pacific.

General
Last of the Curlews, F. Bodsworth (Dodd, Mead, New York, 1954), 128 pp.
Hawks Aloft, M. Broun (Dodd, Mead, New York, 1948), 222 pp.
The Last Passenger, J. R. Johnson (Macmillan, New York, 1956), 116 pp.
An Introduction to Birds, J. Kieran (Doubleday, New York, 1950), 77 pp.
Birds Over America, R. T. Peterson (Dodd, Mead, New York, 1948), 342 pp.
The Bird Watcher's Anthology, same (Harcourt, Brace, New York, 1957), 401 pp.
Wild America, Peterson & Fisher (Houghton Mifflin, Boston, 1955), 434 pp.

Life Histories
Life Histories of North American Birds, A. C. Bent (U.S. National Museum, Washington, 1919-58), 20 vols.
Bent's Life Histories of North American Birds, Abridged, H. H. Collins, Jr. (Harpers, New York, 1960) 2 vols.: Water Birds, Land Birds.

Migration
The Migration of North American Birds, F. Lincoln (Doubleday, New York, 1952), 102 pp.

Nests
Birds' Nests, R. Headstrom (Washburn, New York, 1949), 128 pp.
Birds' Nests of the West, same, 1951, 177 pp.

Photographing Birds
Hunting with the Camera, A. D. Cruickshank and others (Harpers, New York, 1957), 215 pp.

Regional and Foreign
A Field Guide to the Birds of Britain and Europe, R. T. Peterson, E. Mountfort, P.A.D. Hollom (Houghton Mifflin, Boston, 1954) 318 pp.
Birds of Mexico, E. R. Blake (Chicago Univ. Press, Chicago, 1953), 644 pp.
Birds of the West Indies, J. Bond (Houghton Mifflin, 1961), 256 pp.
A Natural History of the Birds of Eastern & Central North America, Forbush & May (Houghton Mifflin, Boston, 1939), 554 pp., 97 excellent color plates by Fuertes and others; west to the Plains.
Birds of Canada, P. A. Taverner (Musson, Toronto, 1949), 446 pp.

Song
A Guide to Bird Songs, A. A. Saunders, (Doubleday, New York, 1951), 307 pp.

Taxidermy
The Preparation of Birds for Study, Science Guide no. 58, J. P. Chapin (Am. Mus. Nat. Hist, New York, 1946), 48 pp.

The lesser scaup is a diving duck. It dives below the surface of the water for its food.
Helen Cruickshank—National Audubon Society

Textbooks

Laboratory and Field Manual of Ornithology, O. S. Pettingill (Burgess, Minneapolis, 1956), 379 pp.

Fundamentals of Ornithology, Van Tyne & Berger (Wiley, New York, 1959), 624 pp.

An Introduction to Ornithology, G. J. Wallace (Macmillan, New York, 1955), 443 pp.

Natural History of Birds, L. W. Wing (Ronald, New York, 1956), 539 pp.

State Bird Books

Many state and provincial bird books have been published over the years. The one for your state or province will tell what birds you are likely to see, where they may be seen, and when. Some of these books are quite comprehensive; others are merely annotated check lists. Several rank among the classics of ornithology.

Alabama, Birds of, A. H. Howell (Dept. of Game & Fisheries, Montgomery, 1928)

Alaska, Birds of, Gabrielson & Lincoln (Stackpole, Harrisburg, Pa., 1959)

Arizona and Its Bird Life, H. Brandt (Bird Research Foundation, Cleveland, O., 1951)

Arkansas, Birds of, W. J. Baerg (U. of Ark. Experiment Station, Fayetteville, 1931)

California, The Birds of, W. L. Dawson (Cooper Ornithological Society, 1923)

Colorado. *The Birds of Denver and the Mountain Parks*, Niedrach & Rockwell (Col. Mus. Nat. Hist., Denver, 1939)

Connecticut. See Massachusetts

Delaware. See Maryland

District of Columbia. See Maryland

Florida Bird Life, A. Sprunt, Jr. (Coward-McCann, New York, 1954)

Georgia Birds, T. D. Burleigh (U. of Okla. Press, 1958)

Hawaiian Birds (Hawaiian Audubon Society, Honolulu)

Idaho, A Check-list of the Birds of, M. D. Arvey (U. of Kan. Mus. Nat. Hist., Lawrence, Kansas, 1947)

Illinois, Check List of the Birds of, Smith & Parmelee (Illinois State Museum, Springfield, Illinois, 1955)

The curved-billed thrasher is found in the deserts of the Southwest, where it nests in cacti.

Helen Cruickshank—National Audubon Society

The western grebe, our largest grebe, nests among reeds in fresh water.

Indiana Birds (Indiana Dept. of Conservation, Indianapolis, 1948)

Iowa, List of the Birds of, P. A. Dumont (U. of Ia., Iowa City, Ia., 1934)

Kansas, Check-list of the Birds of, H. B. Tordoff (U. of Kansas, Lawrence, 1956)

Louisiana Birds, G. H. Lowery, Jr. (La. State Univ. Press, Baton Rouge, 1954)

Maine Birds, R. S. Palmer (Mus. Comp. Zool., Cambridge, Mass.)

Maryland. *Birds of Maryland & the District of Columbia*, Stewart & Robbins (Fish & Wildlife Service, Washington, 1958)

Massachusetts. *The Birds of Massachusetts and Other New England States*, E. H. Forbush (Mass. Dept. of Agric., Boston, 1925-9), 3 vols.

Michigan, Check List of the Birds of, J. Van Tyne (Mich. Mus. Zool., Ann Arbor, 1938)

Minnesota, The Birds of, T. S. Roberts (U. of Minn. Press, Minneapolis, 1937)

Missouri, Check-List of the Birds of, R. Bennitt (U. of Mo. Studies VII, 1932)

Montana, Birds of, A. A. Saunders (Mus. Vert. Zool., Berkeley, Calif., 1921)

Nebraska, Check-list of the Birds of, Haecker, Moser & Swenk (Neb. State Mus., Lincoln, 1945)

Nevada, Birds of, J. M. Linsdale (Mus. of Vert. Zool., Berkeley, Calif., 1936)

New Hampshire. See Massachusetts

New Jersey Birds, D. Fables Jr. (Urner Orn. Club, Newark Mus., Newark, 1955). *Bird Studies at Old Cape May*, W. Stone (Del. Valley Orn. Club, Ac. Nat. Sciences, Philadelphia, 1937), 2 vols.

New Mexico, Birds of, F. M. Bailey (N.M. Dept. Fish & Game, Santa Fe, 1928)

New York, Birds of, E. H. Eaton (State Mus., Albany, 1923) 2 vols. *Birds of the New York City Area*, J. Bull (Am. Mus. Nat. Hist., New York, 1958)

North Carolina, Birds of, Pearson, Brimley and Brimley (State Mus., Raleigh, 1942)

North Dakota, Survey of the Bird Life of, N. A. Wood (Mich. Mus. Zool., Ann Arbor, Mich., 1923)

Ohio, A Check List of the Birds of, D. J. Borror (Dept. Zool., Ohio State U., Columbus, 1950)

Oklahoma, Birds of, M. M. Nice (U. of Okla. Press, Norman, 1924)

Oregon, Birds of, Gabrielson & Jewett (Ore. State College, Corvallis, 1940)

Pennsylvania, Birds of Western, W. E. C. Todd (U. of Pittsburgh Press, 1940)

Rhode Island. See Massachusetts

South Carolina Bird Life, Sprunt & Chamberlain (University of South Carolina Press, Columbia, 1949)

This Carolina wren has built its nest in a clothespin bag.

South Dakota, Birds of, Over & Thoms (U. of S.D. Mus., Vermillion, 1946)

Tennessee, List of the Birds of, A. F. Ganier (Tenn. Orn. Soc., Nashville, 1933)

A Field Guide to the Birds of Texas, R. T. Peterson (Pub. for Texas Game & Fish Commission by Houghton Mifflin, 1960)

Texas Bird Adventures, H. Brandt (Bird Research Foundation, Cleveland, O., 1940)

Utah, Check-list of the Birds of, Woodbury, Cottam & Sugden (U. of Utah, Salt Lake City, 1949)

Vermont. See Massachusetts

Virginia, A Check List of the Birds of, J. J. Murray (Williamsburg, 1952)

Washington. *Birds of Washington State,* Jewett and others (U. of Wash. Press, Seattle, 1953)

West Virginia, A Check List of Birds, M. Brooks (Agricultural Experiment Station, West Va. University, Morgantown, W. Va., 1944)

Wisconsin Birds, Barger and others (Wis. Soc. of Orn., Conservation Dept., Madison, 1942)

Wyoming Bird Life, O. McCreary (Burgess, Minneapolis, 1939)

Newfoundland, Birds of, Peters & Burleigh (Houghton Mifflin, Boston, 1951)

Canada, Arctic Birds of, L. L. Snyder (University of Toronto Press, 1957). *Ontario, Breeding Birds in,* Baillie & Harrington (Royal Ontario Museum of Zoology, Toronto, Ontario, Canada, 1937)

Bird Club Publications in the U.S. and Canada

Atlantic Naturalist (Audubon Naturalist Society), Shirley A. Briggs, Editor, Box 202, Benjamin Franklin Station, Washington 4, D.C.

Audubon Bulletin (Illinois Audubon Society), Paul H. Lobik, Editor, 22 W. 681 Tamarack Drive, Glen Ellyn, Ill.

Audubon Magazine (National Audubon Society), 1130 5th Avenue, N.Y.C. 28, N.Y.

Audubon Outlook (Buffalo Audubon Society), Mrs. Elek D. Csont, Editor, Beach Avenue, Athol Springs, N.Y.

Auk (American Ornithologists' Union), c/o Division of Birds, National Museum, Washington 25, D.C.

Blue Jay (Saskatchewan Natural History Society), George F. Ledingham, 2335 Athol St., Regina, Saskatchewan, Canada

Canadian Audubon (Audubon Society of Canada), Mrs. Jean Hart Whittemore, Editor, 4235 Sherbourne St., Toronto 5, Canada

Chat (Carolina Bird Club), Charles H. Blake, Editor (Distribution Office, N.C. State Museum, Box 2281, Raleigh, N.C.)

Condor (Cooper Ornithological Society), c/o O. V. Duff, Bus. Mgr., 2911 Antelo View Dr., Los Angeles 24, Calif.

Flicker (Minnesota Ornithologists' Union), Museum of Natural History, University of Minnesota, Minneapolis, Minn.

Florida Naturalist (Florida Audubon Society), C. Russell Mason, Editor, P.O. Box 821, Maitland, Florida

Indiana Audubon Quarterly, James B. Cope, Editor, Earlham College, Richmond, Indiana

Iowa Bird Life (Iowa Ornithologists' Union), Fred J. Pierce, Editor, Winthrop, Iowa

Jack Pine Warbler (Michigan Audubon Society), Harrison B. Tordoff, Editor, Museum of Zoology, University of Michigan, Ann Arbor, Mich.

Kentucky Warbler (Kentucky Ornithological Society), Dr. Gordon Wilson, Editor, 1434 Chestnut St., Bowling Green, Kentucky

Kingbird (Federation of New York State Bird Clubs), Minnie B. Scotland, Editor, 42 Continental Avenue, Cohoes, N.Y.

Linnaean Society Newsletter (The Linnaean Society of New York), c/o American Museum of Natural History, New York City

Maine Field Naturalist (Maine Audubon Society and Portland Society of Natural History), Editors: Alfred O. Gross, 11 Boody St., Brunswick, Maine, Christopher M. Packard, Portland Society of Natural History, 22 Elm St., Portland, Maine

Maryland Birdlife (Maryland Ornithological Society), Chandler S. Robbins, Editor, Patuxent Refuge, Laurel, Maryland

Massachusetts Audubon Society Bulletin, Elmer Foye, Editor, Drumlin Farm, South Lincoln, Mass.

Migrant (Tennessee Ornithological Society), Lee R. Herndon, Editor, 1533 Burgie Place, Elizabethton, Tennessee

Nebraska Bird Review (Nebraska Ornithologists' Union), Doris B. Gates, Editor, Nebraska State Teachers College, Chadron, Nebraska

New Hampshire Bird News (Audubon Society of New Hampshire), Mrs. Ralph Brainard, Editor, Walpole, New Hampshire

New Jersey Nature News (New Jersey Audubon Society), Frank W. McLaughlin, Exec. Dir., Ewing Avenue, Franklin Lakes, N.J.

Oriole (Georgia Ornithological Society), David W. Johnston, Editor, Department of Biology, Mercer University, Macon, Ga.

Passenger Pigeon (Wisconsin Society for Ornithology), Samuel D. Robbins, Editor, Adams, Wisconsin

Raven (Virginia Society of Ornithology), Rev. J. J. Murray, Editor, Lexington, Va.

Redstart (Brooks Bird Club), George A. Hall, Editor, Department of Chemistry, West Virginia University, Morgantown, W. Va.

South Dakota Bird Notes (South Dakota Ornithologists' Union), J. S. Findley, Editor, 1201 South Center Avenue, Sioux Falls, S.D.

Warbler (Des Moines Audubon Society), Gladys Heifner Haskell, Editor, 231 East Creston Avenue, Des Moines, Iowa

Wilson Bulletin (Wilson Ornithological Society), c/o Museum of Zoology, Ann Arbor, Mich.

This laughing gull is in summer plumage. In winter its head is white with a black smudge.

Helen Cruickshank—National Audubon Society

INDEX

*Page numbers in **boldface** indicate pages where subjects are illustrated.*

These are the principal migration routes, or flyways, of birds in the United States. The birds travel north in the spring; south in the fall.